Reformed Baptist Covenant Theology

"With historical awareness, exegetical attention, and pastoral sensitivity, *Reformed Baptist Covenant Theology* will serve God's people as a helpful overview of the Reformed Baptist articulation of covenant theology. I commend it to anyone who wants to know how the Bible fits together, how the covenants relate, and how the church fits into God's redemptive plan."

—JON ENGLISH LEE
Pastor of Discipleship, Morningview Baptist Church

"We are greatly indebted to Phillip Griffiths for outlining a Reformed Baptist understanding of the covenant of grace and its implications for us as new-covenant believers in Christ. With a biblical covenant theology to guide our understanding of the church, we can really enjoy all the blessings of being new-covenant believers gathered in our congregations each Lord's Day to revel in *all* the benefits of the fullness of covenant grace in Christ Jesus."

—OLIVER ALLMAND-SMITH
Pastor, Trinity Grace Church

"Griffiths provides the reader a clear and easy-to-read overview of the major covenants of the Old Testament and their place in God's providence to redeem his people . . . *Reformed Baptist Covenant Theology* will help the reader see the purpose of God in the often-neglected left side of his Bible."

—KARL MINOR
Pastor, Christ Reformed Baptist Fellowship

"For anyone who has struggled to articulate the distinction between the old covenant God made with Moses and the new covenant made through Christ, this book is for you . . . God has blessed Griffiths with a clear mind to untangle and explain in a simple, clear way what Baptists have always believed. Anyone reading this book will find themselves giving thanks to God in their heart, liberated in their Christian life and more solid in their understanding of the promises of God."

—**C. P. REES**
Minister, Bethesda Chapel

"I feel like a child in understanding the covenants and their relationships with one another. It is helpful to read the views of someone who has sought to come to grips with this challenging matter."

—**GEOFF THOMAS**
Retired Minister, Alfred Place Baptist Church

Reformed Baptist Covenant Theology

Phillip D. R. Griffiths

RESOURCE *Publications* · Eugene, Oregon

REFORMED BAPTIST COVENANT THEOLOGY

Copyright © 2022 Phillip D. R. Griffiths. All rights reserved. Except for brief quotations in critical publications or reviews, no part of this book may be reproduced in any manner without prior written permission from the publisher. Write: Permissions, Wipf and Stock Publishers, 199 W. 8th Ave., Suite 3, Eugene, OR 97401.

Resource Publications
An Imprint of Wipf and Stock Publishers
199 W. 8th Ave., Suite 3
Eugene, OR 97401

www.wipfandstock.com

PAPERBACK ISBN: 978-1-6667-1715-0
HARDCOVER ISBN: 978-1-6667-1716-7
EBOOK ISBN: 978-1-6667-1717-4

02/24/22

Scripture quotations are from The Holy Bible, English Standard Version (ESV), copyright © 2001 by Crossway. Used by permission. All rights reserved.

Contents

Introduction | vii

1. What is a Covenant | 1
2. The Plight of Humanity Under the First Man | 4
3. Redemption through the Second Adam | 12
4. The New Covenant in the Old Testament | 21
5. Application of New Covenant Before Abraham | 37
6. Promissory Covenant with Abraham | 42
7. The Covenant of Circumcision | 51
8. Abraham's Double Capacity | 63
9. The Sinaitic Covenant | 75
10. The Davidic Covenant | 102
11. Circumcision and Baptism? | 108
12. The Distinguishing Factor | 127

Conclusion | 133
Bibliography | 135
Scripture Index | 139

Introduction

THE WRITER TELLS US that 'of making many books there is no end, and much study is a weariness of the flesh' (Eccl 12:12). In the annals of church history there has never been so much knowledge available to Christians, yet we live in an age where relatively few experience the weariness that results from much study. Many Christians simply do not seek to delve deeply into the Faith. The majority who attend Baptist churches have given little thought to what being a Baptist means, and, when pressed, they associate it with the mode of baptism and the fact that the rite is only performed on those who have made a profession of faith. Not only this, but many have been unduly swayed by the 1647 Westminster Confession of Faith rather than the 1689 Baptist Confession. This has resulted in a covenant theology which is essentially a tinkered version of Presbyterianism.

Thankfully, in recent years there has been a resurgent interest in exactly what it means to be a Reformed Baptist. There has consequently been a spate of books examining the Baptist understanding of the covenants. This being the case one might well ask why it is necessary to write yet another book on this? Many previous books, like my earlier book[1], have adopted a polemical stance.

---

1. *Covenant Theology: A Reformed Baptist Perspective.*

Introduction

They have sought to show why paedobaptism[2] is wrong as much as they have sought to explain credobaptism. In this book, I seek to be more positive. Having said this, I do touch upon the areas of disagreement, but only in so far as this assists me in explicating the Reformed Baptist position. I also, when the need arises, seek to answer some of the criticisms levelled at our position.

I am well aware that there are those Reformed paedobaptists who believe the term "Reformed Baptist" is something of a misnomer. This is because we do not tick every box, because we have a different understanding of the covenants and ecclesiology from that of the reformed tradition. Should we be worried about this? Certainly not. We believe in the five solas[3] of the Reformation, in election and predestination etc. The Reformers were not perfect, like all sinful men, they had feet of clay. They simply failed to go far enough in their covenant theology and continued to place the children of believers in the new covenant.

It is important to stress from the outset that on the essentials of the Faith, Reformed Baptists[4] stand shoulder to shoulder with their Reformed paedobaptist brethren. Indeed, apart from church government and covenant theology, the 1689 London Baptist Confession is virtually the same as the 1647 Westminster Confession and the 1658 Savoy Confession.

It is for this reason I quote from paedobaptists. Reformed Baptists are indebted to men like John Owen, whose views of the Mosaic covenant fit into the Baptist paradigm. Indeed, Reformed Baptist, Nehemiah Coxe, after his work on the Abrahamic covenant, was going to write about the Mosaic covenant. His reason for not doing so was, in his own words:

> I designed to give a further account of it in a discourse of the covenant made with Israel in the wilderness and the state of the church under the law. But when I had finished this and provided some materials also for what was

2. A paedobaptist is one who believes in infant baptism.
3. *Sola scriptura; Sola fide; Sola gratia; Solus Christus; Soli Deo gloria.*
4. Reformed Baptists are also known as Particular or Calvinistic Baptists because they espouse a Calvinistic soteriology.

Introduction

to follow, I found my labor for the clearing and asserting of that point happily prevented by the coming out of Dr. Owen's third volume on Hebrews. There it was discussed at length and the objections that seem to lie against it are fully answered, especially in the exposition of the eighth chapter. I now refer my reader there for satisfaction about it which he will find commensurate to what might be expected from so great and learned a person.[5]

So even though Owen adopted a different position from that of the Baptists regarding the place of children in the covenant, he adopted a view of the old covenant that rings true for Baptists.

Having said this, the role of baptism in the church is not a minor issue, as Wellum reminds us, "the baptismal question is a major test-case for one's entire theological system, since it tells us much about how one puts the entire canon together."[6] We all agree that unity in the body of Christ is vital, it must, however, be based upon theological integrity. It must not be sacrificed; the theological differences must not be blurred for the sake of unity. Regarding infant baptism, Paul Jewett opined that *"To baptize infants apart from faith threatens the evangelical foundations of evangelicalism."*[7] The practice of baptizing infants and categorizing them as church members, those that belong to the body of Christ, severs the all-important connection between faith and church admittance. It is only believers' baptism that accords with Scripture because "it teaches that the objective work of God in salvation necessarily leads to the subjective response of faith."[8]

For several years after becoming a Christian, while I attended a Baptist church, I had little appreciation of the Baptist position regarding covenant theology. I believed being a Baptist simply meant that one should only be baptized upon a profession of faith and that the mode of baptism should involve full immersion. I unquestionably, and unknowingly, accepted Presbyterian covenant theology,

---

5. Coxe, *A Discourse of the Covenants*, 30.
6. Wellum, "Relationship Between the Covenants" 160.
7. Jewett, *Infant Baptism and the Covenant of Grace*, 162
8. Shreiner and Wright, "Introduction," in *Believer's Baptism*, 2.

Introduction

namely, that there is one covenant of grace with two administrations, i.e., the old and new covenants. I then tinkered with this in an attempt to make it fit into a Baptist framework. I failed to appreciate the essential fact that there is a substantial and qualitative distinction between the old and new covenants. Instead of all salvific blessings flowing out of the new covenant alone, I was wrongly attributing the old covenant with an efficacy it never possessed.

Over time I became particularly concerned about two Old Testament passages which, in spite of having tried, I simply could not reconcile with the twofold administration of the one covenant of grace. In Jeremiah 31:31–34 we read:

> Behold, the days are coming, declares the Lord, when I will make a new covenant with the house of Israel and the house of Judah, not like the covenant that I made with their fathers on the day when I took them by the hand to bring them out of the land of Egypt, my covenant that they broke, though I was their husband, declares the Lord. For this is the covenant that I will make with the house of Israel after those days, declares the Lord: I will put my law within them, and I will write it on their hearts. And I will be their God, and they shall be my people. And no longer shall each one teach his neighbor and each his brother, saying, 'Know the Lord,' for they shall all know me, from the least of them to the greatest, declares the Lord. For I will forgive their iniquity, and I will remember their sin no more.

Again, the prophet Ezekiel speaks about God giving his people a new heart of flesh and placing his Spirit within them, thereby causing them to walk in his statutes (Ezek 36: 26–27). Both of these passages depict these blessings as applying only to the new covenant.

The Presbyterians tell us that the new covenant is not really new, but is rather a qualitative improvement on what had gone before, that it is a brighter, richer and fuller revelation, but, in regards to its substance, it is the same as the old covenant. A typical example of the "newness" of the new covenant is provided by Jonty Rhodes:

Introduction

> The word "new" can be a bit misleading. Take two examples: "I'm going to build a new house," and "He's become a new man since he married." In the first example, new means "never existed before." In the second, it has more the sense of "renewed" or "dramatically changed for the better." It is in this second sense that the new covenant is "new." It is not a completely new creation unrelated to what has gone before.[9]

In other words, the blessings which we associate with the new covenant were then applied to Old Testament saints, not because they were in the new covenant, recipients of its blessings, but because the old covenant was just an earlier administration of the covenant of grace, containing the same blessings.

From reading Jeremiah 31 and Hebrews 8:8–13, it became patently clear that there are no "ifs" or "buts," the blessings referred to in these passages are specifically for those in the new covenant. Yet if the blessings of the new covenant were not given to the church until New Testament times, after its formal ratification, how could these blessings have applied to those who lived before Christ? Did not Abraham, for example, know the LORD? Did he not have a new heart and God's Spirit within him? How could he, and other Old Testament believers, have these when the new covenant, the only covenant with which these blessings are associated, still lay in the future? The Presbyterian answer, namely, that these blessings were applicable outside the new covenant simply made no sense.

The Reformed Baptist answer to this is simply that Old Testament saints were recipients of these blessings because, although the new covenant's ratification lay in the future sacrificial death of the lamb, the blessings associated with it were applied retroactively to those who believed in the promised Christ. By laying hold of the promise, saints like Abraham were made participators in Christ, sharing in the same blessings as their New Testament counterparts. Old Testament believers were then, through faith in the promise, effectively members of the new covenant on account of its backward reaching efficacy.

---

9. Rhodes, *Covenants Made Simple*, 95–96.

Introduction

Understanding God's covenants is essential for understanding Scripture. As the skeleton holds together the body, so God's covenants provide form to the Scriptures. The great 19th century Baptist, Charles Haddon Spurgeon went so far as to say "the doctrine of covenants is the key of theology."[10] One cannot rightly divide God's word without grasping the essential difference between the old and new covenants. One will simply end up, to use the proverbial saying, "missing the wood for the trees." To quote Wellum:

> One cannot fully understand Scripture and correctly draw theological conclusions from it without grasping how all the biblical covenants unfold across time and find their telos, terminus, and fulfilment in Christ . . . we assert the covenants form the backbone of the Bible's metanarrative and thus it is essential to "put them together" correctly in order to discern accurately the "whole counsel of God (Acts 20:27)."[11]

Or as Walter Chantry puts it:

> Marrow is at the center of the bones which shape our body, and marrow gives health to the body. So the doctrine of the covenants is at the core of theology, and the health of any theological system depends on its understanding of this truth. It would be nearly impossible to overstate the central importance of the biblical teaching on covenants.[12]

For me, coming to understand the Reformed Baptist view of God's covenants was a kind of eureka moment. As we shall see, it is marked by elegant simplicity.

It should be emphasized that "The paedobaptist position is not one monolithic thing, but a variety of approaches to the question of infant baptism."[13] In the following, when I refer to

---

10. Spurgeon, *The Early Years*, 39.
11. Wellum et al, *God's Kingdom through God's Covenants*, 17
12. Chantry, "The Covenants of Grace and of Works," 89.
13. Rainbow, " 'Confessor Baptism' The Baptismal Doctrine of the Early Anabaptists" 204.

Introduction

paedobaptists I will have in mind those of a Reformed persuasion, in particular, Reformed Presbyterians—those who hold with the 1647 Westminster Confession of Faith. Hence, I will use Reformed paedobaptist and Presbyterian interchangeably.

Many people today seem averse to using theological terms, e.g., justification by faith, sanctification, covenant theology, etc. Even preachers, instead of teaching the biblical meaning of the various terms, will go out of their way to use alternative expressions. I'm sure the reason for this is the superficiality that marks the present age. People no longer seem willing to put in the necessary effort to secure understanding. I make no apology for using theological terminology. In the words of Gresham Machen:

> Many persons are horrified by the use of a theological term; they seem to have the notion that modern Christians must be addressed always in words of one syllable, and that in religion we must abandon the scientific precision of language which is found to be useful in other spheres [e.g., medicine, science, technology, economics, history, art, etc] . . . I am perfectly ready, indeed, to agree that the Bible and the modern man ought to be brought together. But what is not always observed is that there are two ways of attaining that end. One way is to bring the Bible down to the level of the modern man; but the other way is to bring the modern man up to the level of the Bible. For my part, I am inclined to advocate the latter way. And I am by no means ready to relinquish the advantages of a precise terminology in summarizing Bible truth. In religion as well as in other spheres a precise terminology is mentally economical in the end; it repays amply the slight effort for the mastery of it.[14]

In what follows, I will first briefly look at what is meant by a covenant, before examining the two primary covenants and their respective heads, namely, Adam and Christ. Here it will be necessary to examine the consequences for humanity of Adam's disobedience, showing that all are by nature under the covenant of works, before examining the blessings that belong to those under

14. Machen, *What is Faith*, 162–63.

Introduction

the headship of Christ in the new covenant. This will be followed with an examination of the application of the blessings procured by Christ, both prior to and after the new covenant's ratification. I will then look at the nature of the subsidiary covenants, those made with Abraham, Moses, and David, showing how they were subservient to the promise of the new covenant; serving to make the promise more prominent. I will then look at exactly who should be baptized. Finally, I will examine the nature of the blessing that was first bestowed on the church at Pentecost. Here I hope to show how it is this blessing that essentially separates New Testament believers from their Old Testament counterparts.

1
———

What is a Covenant

BEFORE WE CAN GO any further we need to determine exactly what a covenant is. There is much that could be written about this. For this work, however, it will be necessary to provide only a basic understanding.

"Covenant" is unquestionably one of the most important words used in the Bible. The Hebrew word for covenant is *Berith*, which occurs no less than 275 times. The Greek word is *Diatheke*, and this occurs thirty-three times. Our Bible is divided into two sections, the Old and New Testaments. The word 'testament' is simply another name for covenant. The Old Testament, however, is not synonymous with the old covenant, although most of what we read about from the Old Testament is concerned with the old covenant. By Old Testament is meant the entire contents of the Scriptures revealed before the first advent, i.e., the 39 books, ranging from Genesis to Malachi. The old covenant, as used in Scripture refers to the covenant made with Moses, which we usually refer to as the Mosaic or Sinaitic covenant.

One usually considers a covenant to be an agreement or a contract. When made between two equal parties it is, in the words of paedobaptist A. A. Hodge, "a mutual understanding and the agreement of two wills."[1] The covenants that God has made with

---

1. Hodge, A. A. *Evangelical Theology*, 166.

man are different from covenants made between men because they are made between a superior party (God) and an inferior party (man). It is important to bear in mind that "in the Bible a divine covenant is never a pact resulting from bargaining or mutual discussion . . . A divine covenant is always a unilateral, one-sided imposition."[2] Or as Berkhof puts it:

> God and man do not appear as equals in any of these covenants. All God's covenants are of the nature of sovereign dispositions imposed on man. God is absolutely sovereign in His dealings with man, and has the perfect right to lay down the conditions which the latter must meet, in order to enjoy His favor.[3]

Such covenants are not "the product of human request or cajoling. It comes from the free, spontaneous activity of God."[4] A covenant made by God is "an unchangeable divinely imposed legal agreement between God and man that stipulates the conditions of their relationship."[5] These covenants are essentially conditional promises. God promises blessings if the covenantal conditions are kept and he threatens curses if they are broken. For example, in Deuteronomy chapter 28 we have a list of blessings for the nation's obedience to the covenant (vv.1–14) and a list of the curses (vv.15ff) for disobedience.

There are also what might be called 'unconditional' covenants in Scripture. A good example is God's covenant with Noah and his descendants in Genesis 8:20—9:17. Here there are no conditions imposed upon man, but only God's promise to never again destroy all life. As we shall see later, we find the same kind of covenant in Genesis 15, where again no conditions are stipulated. We may, in the words of Waldron, define this type of covenant as "a sworn promise—a commitment certified by an oath."[6]

---

2. Waldron, *A Modern Exposition of the 1689 Baptist Confession of Faith*, 115.

3. Berkhof, *Systematic Theology*, 213.

4. Berkhof, *Systematic Theology*, 116.

5. Grudem, *Systematic Theology*, 515.

6. Waldron, *A Mordern Exposition of the 1689 Baptist Confession of Faith*, 117.

What is a Covenant

Although there is much more that can be said about the biblical covenants, the above should suffice for what I have to say here.

2

The Plight of Humanity Under the First Man

ALTHOUGH THE SCRIPTURES MENTION several different covenants, there are only two primary covenants. The first covenant in time was the covenant of works made with Adam, the first man. The second covenant, what we call the new covenant, while it was revealed to humanity after the covenant of works, is the outworking, in time, of a covenant made in eternity. This eternal covenant is what theologians refer to as the covenant of redemption.[1] It is essentially an agreement made between the three Persons of the Godhead before creation itself. The new covenant is essentially the operational stage of this covenant. Let me use a simply analogy. Let us assume that a difficult military operation is to be undertaken. First there is the planning stage, where what will happen, who will do what etc., is determined. Everything is worked out to the smallest detail before the operation itself. When this has been done the plan will be executed, put into action or operation. So it is with the covenant of redemption and the new covenant. The former is the planning stage which occurred before creation, while the latter is the execution of the plan in time. Both of these covenants are

---

1. Scripture does not use the term covenant of redemption. It can, however, be gleaned from what it does say that the Father, Son and Holy Spirit each have a specific role to play in man's redemption.

The Plight of Humanity Under the First Man

essentially one; together they are what Scripture calls "the everlasting covenant" (Heb 13:20).

The sole purpose of all other covenants, which are essentially subsidiary covenants, is to facilitate the primary covenant whose mediator is Jesus Christ; this is called the new covenant. This will all become clear as we proceed.

The first covenant[2] was made with Adam in the Garden of Eden. Although it was not specifically called a covenant it had all the hallmarks of being one:

> There was an original covenant made with Adam, and all mankind in him. The rule of obedience and reward that was between God and him was not expressly called a covenant, but it *contained the express nature of a covenant; for it was the agreement of God and man concerning obedience and disobedience, rewards and punishments.*[3]

In Genesis 2:16–17 we read:

> And the Lord God commanded the man, saying, "You may surely eat of every tree of the garden, but of the tree of the knowledge of good and evil you shall not eat, for in the day that you eat of it you shall surely die."

The two parties to the covenant were God and Adam. The covenantal condition was obedience. Adam, being made in the image and after the likeness of God (Gen 1:26), had the law of God written upon his heart. The Second London Baptist Confession tells us that "God gave to Adam a law of universal obedience written in his heart, and a particular precept of not eating of the tree of knowledge of good and evil." About this law, Reformed Baptist, John Gill states:

---

2. While I call this the first covenant it would be more precise to say that the first covenant was that made between the Persons of the Godhead, where the Father gave a people to the Son, a people for whom the Son agreed to perform his work of redemption. This was a covenant made before time and is usually referred to as The Covenant of Redemption.

3. Owen, *Works* Vol. 22, 60.

> The law given to him was both of a natural and positive kind. God who is the creator of all, Judge of all the earth, and King of the whole world, has the right to give what laws He likes to his creatures, and they are bound as creatures, and by ties of gratitude, to observe them. The natural law, or law of nature, given to Adam, was concreated with him, written on his heart, and engraved and imprinted in his nature from the beginning of his existence, by which he was acquainted with the will of his maker, and directed to observe it.[4]

Although it is not explicitly stated, the blessing of the covenant was eternal life. While Adam was created in original righteousness there was still the possibility of falling into sin and dying. The possession of immortality[5] was dependent on his obedience. The penalty or curse for disobedience was death. This death essentially meant separation from God. Shortly after Adam sinned God banished him from the Garden and set cherubim at the entrance with a flaming sword (Gen 3:24). This casting out from God's presence is man's spiritual death. Man was from that moment separated and estranged from God. Physical death also became a reality.

The covenant with the first man is called the covenant of works because it is based upon Adam's own obedience. So important is this covenant that Wilhelmus a Brakel writes:

> Acquaintance with this covenant is of the greatest importance, for whoever errs here or denies the existence of the covenant of works, will not understand the covenant of grace, and will readily err concerning the mediatorship of the Lord Jesus. Such a person will very readily deny that Christ by His active obedience has merited a right to eternal life for the elect.[6]

This is because the covenant which Jesus kept was also the covenant of works that Adam broke. In explaining what Christ achieved, the Apostle sets it against what Adam lost (Rom 5:12–21).

---

4. Gill, *Body of Divinity, Vol.1*, 444.
5. Immortality essentially means life in the presence of God.
6. Wilhelmus a Brakel, *The Christian's Reasonable Service*, 355.

The Plight of Humanity Under the First Man

We don't know how long our first parents remained in their original righteousness, but I don't think it was for long. When Adam partook of the forbidden fruit

> He broke, first, the law of his very being, violating his own nature, which bound him unto owing allegiance to his maker: self now took the place of God. Second, he flouted the law of God, which required perfect and unremitting obedience to the moral Governor of the world. Third, in trampling upon the positive ordinance under which he was placed he broke the covenant, preferring to take his stance alongside his fallen wife.[7]

The entrance of sin did not mean the termination of the covenant, it is as much in force today as it was then, only now, man stands under its curse and there is no possibility of him, without a mediator, keeping its conditions. To quote Nehemiah Coxe:

> Once people have fallen under the guilt of breaching the covenant, they are by their own failure utterly disabled from yielding any acceptable obedience to God on the terms of that covenant which they have violated. Their interest in that covenant relationship is forfeited and lost by them. They are under the penal sanction of the covenant, and have wholly lost their right in its reward.[8]

Concerning this covenant, John Owen states:

> That first covenant made with Adam, had, as to any benefit to be expected from it, with respect to acceptance with God, life, and salvation, ceased long before, even at the entrance of sin. It was not abolished or abrogated by any act of God, as a law, but only made weak and insufficient to its first end, as a covenant.[9]

While man, because of the weakness of the flesh (Rom 8:3), cannot keep the covenant, it is still his responsibility to do so. Man's moral

---

7. Pink, *Divine Covenants*, 40.
8. Cox, *A Discourse of the Covenants*, 39
9. Owen, *Works*, 22, 61.

inability does not in any way nullify or mitigate his moral culpability. As Edward Fisher puts it:

> ... it is true, in every covenant, if either party fail in his duty, and perform not his condition, the other party is thereby freed from his part, but the party failing is not freed from till the other release him; and, therefore, though the Lord be freed from performing his condition, that is, from giving to man eternal life, yet so is not man from his part; no, though strength to obey be lost, yet man having lost it by his own default, the obligation to obedience remains still; so that Adam and his offspring are no more discharged of their duties, because they have no strength to do them, than a debtor is quitted of his bond, because he wants money to pay it.[10]

Adam didn't sin alone. Louis Berkhof tells us that "the guilt of Adam's sin is imputed to all his descendants. Adam suffered the loss of original righteousness, and thereby incurred the divine displeasure. As a result, all his descendants are deprived of original righteousness, and as such the objects of divine wrath."[11] This means that the position of all humanity by nature is dire. We are under the law's curse because of both Adam's original sin and our own actual sins, and we have not the remotest chance of keeping the covenant's requirements. Left to ourselves our position is hopeless.

Adam was humanity's representative, its federal or covenantal head. When he sinned we all sinned in him. As the Apostle reminds us: "Therefore, just as sin came into the world through one man, and death through sin, and so death spread to all men because all sinned" (Rom 5:12). It was through this one man's trespass that we all died (Rom 5:16). As Edward Fisher puts it:

> The very truth is, Adam by his fall threw down our whole nature headlong into the same destruction, and drowned his whole offspring in the same gulf of misery, and the reason is, because, by God's appointment, he was not to stand or fall as a single person only, but as a common

---

10. Fisher, *A Marrow of Modern Divinity*, 39.
11. Berkhof, *Systematic Theology*, 238.

> public person, representing all mankind to come of him: therefore, as all that happiness, all those gifts, and endowments, which were bestowed upon him, were not bestowed on him alone, but also upon the whole nature of man, and as that covenant which was made with him, was made with the whole of mankind; even so he by breaking covenant lost all, as well for us as for himself. As he received all for himself and us, so he lost all both for himself and us.[12]

Because of humanity's union with Adam, when he sinned, "in his righteous judgement God imputes the guilt of the first sin, committed by the head of the covenant, to all those that are federally related to him. And as a result they are born in a deprived and sinful condition as well, and this inherent corruption also involves guilt."[13] In the words of Lloyd-Jones, God:

> said to him: "Adam, I regard you not only the first of a series, not merely in the natural sense of all who are going to come out of you, I constitute you the representative head, the federal head of all humanity; I am going to make a covenant with you, and I am going to deal with you as the representative head of the entire human race of which you will be the progenitor. I intend to make a covenant with you to this effect that every benefit you enjoy will pass upon your progeny.[14]

Or as Arthur Pink puts it:

> The whole human race had a federal standing in Adam. Not only was each of us seminally in his loins the day God created him, but each of us was legally represented by him when God instituted the covenant of works. Adam acted and transacted in that covenant not merely as a private being, but as a public person; not simply as a single individual, but as the surety and sponsor of his race.[15]

---

12. Fisher, *Marrow of Modern Divinity*, 34,35.
13. Berkhof, *Systematic Theology*, 242.
14. Lloyd-Jones, *Romans* 5, 215.
15. Pink, *The Divine Covenants*, 41.

Reformed Baptist Covenant Theology

Prior to the Fall man had "freedom and power to will and to do that which was good and well pleasing to God," yet his will "was mutable, so that he might fall from it."[16] Since the Fall man is now effectively dead in his transgressions and sins, his will is in bondage. The Baptist Confession states:

> Man, by his fall into a state of sin, hath wholly lost all ability of will to any spiritual good accompanying salvation; so as a natural man, being altogether averse from that good, and dead in sin, is not able by his own strength to convert himself, or to prepare himself thereunto.[17]

The Apostle sums up the human condition:

> "None is righteous, no, not one;
> no one understands; no one seeks for God.
> All have turned aside; together
> they have become worthless;
> no one does good, not even one."
> "Their throat is an open grave;
> they use their tongues to
> deceive."
> "The venom of asps is under
> their lips."
> "Their mouth is full of curses
> and bitterness."
> ""Their feet are swift to shed
> blood;
> in their paths are ruin and misery,
> and the way of peace they have not known."
> "There is no fear of God
> before their eyes."
> (Romans 3:11–18)

While fallen man might be free from external constraint, and in this sense be said to have free-will, because the will is the heart choosing, he does not possess to desire to do that which is spiritually good. He is said to be totally deprived and unable to please

---

16. 1689, 9:2.
17. 1689, 9:3.

The Plight of Humanity Under the First Man

God. From the womb, man is estranged from God (Psa 58:3). He was "brought forth in iniquity and in sin" did his "mother conceive" him (Psa 51:5). Man's will is then in bondage because of his heart's hardness. He will choose only to do that which is evil in the Lord's eyes because he is like his father the devil, and in his fallen state he lives according to the devil's desires (John 8:44).

Man, of himself, is doomed. He has broken the covenant and requires one who will do what he is incapable of doing, namely, placate God's wrath against sin and keep perfectly all that God's law demands, i.e., he needs a second Adam or federal head, one who is the very Son of God himself.

3

Redemption through the Second Adam

THE NEW COVENANT IS "the in-breaking of the covenant of redemption into history through the progressive revelation and retroactive application of the New Covenant."[1] This covenant or pact was made between the persons of the Trinity before creation. Its sole purpose was the redemption of a humanity for the glorification of God's name. The Father chose to send his own Son to do all things necessary to procure the salvation of a particular people whom he had chosen in his Son before the foundation of the world (Eph 1:4). Jesus tells us that he was sent by his Father to do his will, "I can do nothing on my own. As I hear, I judge, and my judgment is just, because I seek not my own will but the will of him who sent me" (John 5:30). That certain people were given to him by his Father (John 6:37) and that the will of God is that he secure the salvation of all of these (John 6:36–40).[2] In achieving the redemption of his people the Son did not hold on to his divine prerogatives but emptied himself taking on the form of a servant, in the likeness of men, humbling himself and being obedient to his Father even to the point of dying upon Calvary's cross (Phil 2:7–8). This

---

1. Micah and Samuel Renihan, "Reformed Baptist Covenant Theology and Biblical Theology" in *Recovering a Covenantal Heritage,* 475–506.

2. See also John 10:14–16, 26–28; 17:6–11, 17–21.

covenant, together with its application in time is what the writer to the Hebrews calls the eternal or everlasting covenant (Heb 13:20).

The term "covenant of grace" is not found in Scripture. It is best to think of it as the new covenant before it was formally ratified or consummated in the shed blood of Christ. Before to this time, the new covenant was revealed to sinners through the promise. For example, when we say that Abraham, or any other Old Testament believer, was saved by grace we mean that he believed in the promise of the coming Christ and was made a recipient of the blessings which flow out of Christ's fulfillment of the covenant of works which his Father made with him, i.e., the new covenant.

Although Christ did not appear in human form until the fullness of time had come, in the promise he "appeared immediately after the fall, as Mediator, as the second and final Adam who occupies the place of the first, restores what the latter corrupted, and accomplishes what he failed to do."[3] In an incomprehensible act of condensation the Son took unto himself a human nature, was born of a woman, and perfectly kept the law's requirements for his people (Gal 4:4; Phil 2:6–8). Not only this, but he voluntarily determined to suffer for his people's sins (2 Cor 5:21).

About Christ the Mediator the 1689 Confession states:

> It pleased God, in his eternal purpose, to choose and ordain the Lord Jesus, his only begotten Son, according to the covenant made between them both, to be the mediator between God and man; the prophet, priest, and king; head and savior of the church, the heir of all things, and judge of the world; unto whom he did from all eternity give a people to be his seed and to be by him in time redeemed, called, justified, sanctified, and glorified.[4]

A mediator is a go-between, one who acts to reconcile two or more parties. Jesus stands in-between the two estranged parties, namely, God and the sinner. He alone is the mediator, as Scripture puts it, "there is one mediator between God and man, the man Jesus

---

3. Bavinck, *Reformed Dogmatics*, vol.3 *Sin and Salvation in Christ*, 215.
4. 1689 Baptist Confession of Faith, 8:1.

Reformed Baptist Covenant Theology

Christ" (1Tim 2:5). In his threefold office of priest, prophet and king, he made atonement for his people.

Although the Scriptures do not distinguish between the three offices of Christ, it is nevertheless useful for us to do so because it facilitates our understanding of his redemptive work. When examining these one must remember that "the functions of prophet, priest, and king mutually imply one another: Christ is always a prophetical Priest and a priestly Prophet, and he is always a royal Priest and a priestly King, and together they accomplish one redemption, to which all are equally essential."[5] The old covenant offices of priest, prophet, and king come together in that which they typified, the antitype, who is none other than the person of Christ.

"A priest is a man divinely chosen, qualified, and authorized to appear before God and to act on behalf of men."[6] Under the old covenant, the priest would offer up an animal without blemish (Ex 12:5; Lev 1:10). Such sacrifices were but types of Christ's sacrifice, the one who is the true "lamb of God who takes away the sin of the world (John 1:29), a spotless lamb who saves us through his own shed blood (1 Pet 1:19). Jesus is both the priest and the sacrifice. His entire life was a living sacrifice to his Father on behalf of others. In all his thoughts and actions Jesus perfectly obeyed the law of God. One might say that he was a personification of God's law. His sacrificial life culminated in his sacrificial death, in which he offered up his body on the cross of Calvary, taking his people's sins upon himself, and, in their stead, as their substitute, suffered his Father's holy wrath. He purchased all that is necessary to save those whom his Father had given him. To quote A. A. Hodge, Jesus secured:

> Not merely the forgiveness of sins, but all that we shall ever experience-regeneration, justification, the adoption of sons, fatherly discipline, perseverance, increase of grace, deliverance in death, the resurrection of our bodies, and all the unimaginable beatitudes of heaven,-all these, kingdom and priesthood and glory, are parts of

---

5. 1689 Baptist Confession of Faith, 202.
6. Hodge, A. A. *Evangelical Theology* 208.

Redemption through the Second Adam

"the purchased possession" secured for us through the priesthood of Christ.[7]

It should also be pointed out that Christ has also secured for his people the faith to believe, a faith which results from regeneration (Eph 2:8).

Unlike the priests of old who offered continual sacrifices which were incapable of securing forgiveness, Jesus did not need to enter into the "holies every year with blood not his own" (Heb 9:25), no, he offered "for all time a single sacrifice of sins," he then "sat down at the right hand of God."(Heb 10:12).

A prophet speaks on behalf of God, he is essentially God's mouthpiece, he reveals the will of God to men. Jesus called himself a prophet (Luke 13:33), and the people recognized him as such (Matt 21:11; Luke 7:46; John 3:2 etc.). The prophets of old would declare, "Thus sayeth the Lord," Jesus, however, used the personal pronoun, "I", "I say unto you." Previous prophets attested to the truth, the way and the light, but Jesus is himself the way and the truth and the light (John 14:6).

As King, Jesus reigns in the hearts of his people. His kingdom is presently spiritual in nature. After his second advent, however, it will be both spiritual and physical. I don't know if the teaching is extant, but a few years ago there were those in the church who were propagating the view that one can accept Christ as Savior and not necessarily as Lord. The truth is somewhat different. When one believes upon the name of Christ, one accepts the whole of Christ. As Hodge reminds us:

> From within, the God-man reigns supreme in every Christian heart. It is impossible to accept Christ as our sacrifice and priest without at the same time cordially accepting him as our prophet, absolutely submitting our understanding to his teaching, and accepting him as our King, submitting implicitly our hearts and wills and lives to his sovereign control.[8]

---

7. Hodge, A. A. *Evangelical Theology*, 220.
8. Hodge, A. A. *Evangelical Theology* 233.

There are only two covenant heads. All humanity is by natural birth united to Adam and, therefore, under the legal obligations of the Adamic covenant obligations and under the law's curse because of sin. All who believe in the promise, however, have been born supernaturally by the Holy Spirit and are in the second or last Adam who is Christ. There exists no other possible position. One is either in the first Adam and condemned or one is in Christ and saved. Walter Chantry sums up the two alternative positions available for humanity:

> You live either under the Covenant of Works or the Covenant of Grace. There are none other but these two . . . Under the Covenant of Grace, the identical demand must be met. No lesser obedience will be accepted. Under the Covenant of Works the curse pronounced for sin is death. Man sinned and death must be the result. Under the Covenant of Grace a Mediator must fulfill perfect righteousness for men who cannot provide it for themselves. The Mediator will also die under the curse of the Covenant of Works in place of sinners. The heel of the seed of the woman is bruised, "Christ has redeemed us from the curse of the law, being made a curse for us . . ." (Gal.3:13). He did this not by abolishing the law or by invalidating the Covenant of Works, but by "being made a curse for us." He met all the demands of the Covenant of Works. He fulfilled all its terms.[9]

What Chantry calls the Covenant of Grace is nothing other than the new covenant. Perhaps the first line of the quote would be better if it read: "You live either under the Adamic covenant of works, or under the new covenant in Christ."

All the people of God, throughout all time, are saved because they have been translated from a position in Adam and placed into the kingdom of Jesus Christ (Col 1:13). All who are in Christ constitute a new humanity, and are what Scripture calls "a royal priesthood, a holy nation, a people for his own possession"(1Pet 2:9). They belong not to this fallen world, their citizenship is in heaven (Phil 3:20). To be in Christ is to be under the rule and reign of God,

---

9. Chantry, "The Covenant of Works and Grace," 103.

Redemption through the Second Adam

in other words, in the kingdom of God. By the same token, all those not in Christ, being still in Adam, are in the kingdom of darkness.

The believer's union with Christ is indissoluble, it can never be broken. The old man, the man one used to be in Adam, is dead and gone, he is never coming back. He has been crucified with Christ (Rom 6:6). The law cannot touch the believer because it has already done its worst in Christ. We can say, therefore, that when Christ died, so did we. When he rose, so did we. The believer's union with Christ is such that he is complete in him, as the Apostle puts it, Jesus Christ has become to us "wisdom from God, righteousness and sanctification and redemption"(1Cor1:30). The believer's identification with Christ is such that he is viewed by God the Father in the same way as Christ himself. Edward Fisher nicely contrasts the believer's position in Adam to that of his union with Christ:

> . . . we are to consider, that as Jesus Christ, the second Adam, entered into the same covenant that the first Adam did, so by him was done whatsoever the first Adam had undone. So the case stands thus,- that as whatsoever the first Adam did, or befell him, was reckoned as done by all mankind, and to have befallen them, even so, whatsoever Christ did, or befell him, is to be reckoned as to have been done by believers, and to have befallen them. So that as sin cometh from Adam alone to all mankind, as he in whom all have sinned; so from Jesus Christ alone cometh righteousness unto all that are in him, as he in whom they all have satisfied the justice of God; far as being in Adam and one with him, all did, in him and with him, transgress the commandment of God; even so, in respect to faith, whereby believers are ingrafted into Christ, and spiritually made one with him, they did all, in him and with him, satisfy the justice of God in his death and sufferings.[10]

Briefly, before moving on, let us examine the doctrine of Justification by faith alone. The doctrine which Calvin called "the

---

10. Fisher, *Marrow of Modern Divinity*, 106–7.

Reformed Baptist Covenant Theology

hinge upon which religion turns."[11] Justification is different from other elements of our salvation,[12] like, for example, sanctification, because it occurs outside of the believer. It is a declaration by God concerning one's legal status. It is a verdict in the law court of God whereby the ungodly sinner is pronounced righteous.[13]

God is so holy he cannot so much as look upon evil (Hab 1:13), his nature demands that all sin be punished by death (Rom 6:23). As we have seen, all humanity outside of Christ is under the covenant of works, united with Adam and condemned because of Adam's sin, and also because of their own individual sins. Quite literally, a state of enmity exists between God and the sinner (Rom 5:10). The sinner finds himself in an impossible position. To fix the broken relationship he would not only need to keep God's law perfectly but also find a way to propitiate God, that is, to deal with, to placate God's holy anger against sin. Sinful man can do neither. The only remedy is for God himself to intervene to end the enmity and bring peace and reconciliation. This is exactly what God has done in and through his Son Jesus Christ. When the sinner believes in the gospel, the covenant of works ceases to apply to him:

> . . . the first covenant ceases toward them as to its curse, in all its concerns as a covenant, and obligation to sinless obedience as the condition of life; because both of them are answered by the mediator of the new covenant. But to all those who receive not the grace tended in the promise, but as a law; and that because neither the obedience it requires not the curse which it threatens are answered.[14]

The sinner is translated from his union with Adam and put into union with Christ, and where he once reaped the awful

---

11. Calvin, *Institutes* 3.11.1.

12. Adoption also implies a change in the believer's legal status, and it is important, as we shall see later, to distinguish between one's legal adoption, the change in status, and the Spirit of adoption.

13. It's important to distinguish this from the Roman Catholic view which sees justification as an imparted blessing, one makes the individual righteous.

14. Owen, *Works*, Vol. 22, 61.

consequences of being in Adam, he now reaps the grace which results from being in Christ.

Justification is the legal forensic act in which God declares the sinner just because of the substitutionary work of Jesus Christ, who through his preceptive obedience kept God's law perfectly, and who in his penal obedience took his Father's wrath upon himself at Calvary. In all, he did everything the sinner was incapable of doing. This is how the 1689 Baptist Confession puts it:

> Those whom God effectually calls, he also freely justifies, not by infusing righteousness into them, but by pardoning their sins, and by accounting and accepting their persons as righteous; not for anything wrought in them, or done by them, but for Christ's sake alone; not by imputing faith itself, the act of believing, or any other evangelical obedience to them, as their righteousness; but by imputing Christ's active obedience unto the whole law, and passive obedience in his death for their whole and sole righteousness by faith, which faith they have not of themselves; it is the gift of God.[15]

Such is the nature of the union between Christ and his people, that what belongs to him, i.e., all he accomplished in his redemptive work, becomes theirs. Jesus' righteousness is said to be imputed to the sinner and the sinner's sins are imputed to Christ. There is, as it were, a two-way transaction. It is because of the sinner's position in Christ that God can declare him justified. As Paul puts it, "For our sake he made him to be sin who knew no sin, so that in him, we might become the righteousness of God" (2 Cor 5:21). Again, he says that "I count everything as loss because of the surpassing worth of knowing Christ Jesus my Lord. For his sake I have suffered the loss of all things and count them as rubbish, in order that I may gain Christ and be found in his, not having a righteousness of my own that comes from the law, but that which comes through faith in Christ, the righteousness from God that depends on faith" (Phil 3:8–9). As regards the believer's standing before God, it is, quite literally, as if he has never sinned. He has been clothed in the

---

15. 1689 Baptist Confession of Faith 11:1.

garments of righteousness. When God looks at the sinner he sees not the sin but the righteousness of Christ.

About the liberty that belongs to those in Christ, the Baptist Confessions says:

> The liberty which Christ has purchased for believers under the gospel consists in their freedom from the guilt of sin, the condemning wrath of God, the rigour and curse of the law, and in their being delivered from this present evil world bondage to Satan, and dominion of sin, from the evil afflictions, the feat and sting of death, the victory of the grave, and everlasting damnation: as also in their free access to God, and their yielding obedience unto him, not out of slavish fear, but a child-like love and willing mind.[16]

All of this, and much more, is true of the believer because he is now in union with Jesus Christ.

As we shall see, throughout redemptive history God has been translating his people, those whom he chose in Christ before the foundation of the world (Eph 1:4), from one kingdom into another, from their plight in Adam into the glorious kingdom Christ.

Before we examine how God did this from the giving of the first redemptive promise to the establishment of the new covenant, let us clarify one very important point, namely, that God has throughout redemptive history been saving men and women through the application of new covenant blessings.

---

16. 1689 Baptist Confession of Faith 21:1.

4

The New Covenant in the Old Testament

THE 1689 REFORMED BAPTIST position has often been subject to misrepresentation. This is especially so regarding our understanding of salvation in the Old Testament. In this chapter, as well as examining the nature of some of the misrepresentations, I seek to show that the saints of God have belonged to the new covenant from the very first believer.

We are all guilty of what psychologists call "confirmation bias."[1] When Presbyterians examine the Reformed Baptist paradigm, confirmation bias causes them to interpret what they read according to their particular system or paradigm. Because of their belief that the one covenant of grace has been administered via different covenants, whenever they come upon the term "new covenant" they tend to limit its application to after Christ's completed work. They then insist that Old Testament believers must have been saved by an earlier administration of the one covenant of grace, i.e., the old covenant. And, of course, because of our insistence that none can be saved outside of the new covenant, many conclude that we somehow exempt from its blessings those believers who lived prior to the new covenant's formal consummation

---

1. Confirmation bias is, to quote Britannica, "the tendency to process information by looking for, or interpreting, information that is consistent with one's existing beliefs".

in the shed blood of Christ. For Presbyterians, then, the new covenant is not the only covenant in which salvation is to be found, but is, rather, the last administration of the covenant of grace.

In the following, I provide a number of examples of misrepresentation. The first is from an article by Geoffrey Neill.[2] In the second I look at two articles by R. Scott Clark from his website Heidelblog.net[3] in which he looks at an important difference between Presbyterians and Particular Baptists. I will then briefly show how even Calvin, failing to grasp the application of the new covenant in the Old Testament, was somewhat flummoxed by Hebrews 8:10, and found himself forced to admit to the application of the new covenant prior to Christ.

Although Neil alludes to views held by non-Baptists, namely, Leon Morris and Philip Hughes,[4] I use his examples because his misrepresentation of their position serves to highlight the way the Reformed Baptist position is all too often misunderstood. Neill, I believe, completely misconstrues what Morris and Hughes believe about the position of Old Testament believers. He first quotes Morris:

> The first point is that the new covenant is inward and dynamic: it is written on the hearts and minds of the people. A defect in the old has been its outwardness. It has divinely given laws, indeed; but it was written on tablets of stone (Ex. 32:15–16). The people had not been able to live up to what they knew was the word of God. It remained external.[5]

He goes on to quote Philip Hughes, stating that he too is "similarly incorrect":

---

2. Neill, "The Newness of the New Covenant,"

3. Clark, "One Important Difference Between The Reformed And Some Particular Baptists: God The Son Was In, With, And Under The Types And Shadows," https://heidelblog.net/2020/03/one

4. Both Morris and Hughes were in the Anglican Church.

5. Neill, "Newness of the New Covenant," 134. Quoted from Leon Morris, "Hebrews," in *The Expositor's Bible Commentary*, ed. Frank E. Gaebelein, col.12. Grand Rapids: Zondervan, 1981, 78.

The New Covenant in the Old Testament

> The new covenant, *not like the covenant* made with the people through Moses, would be of grace, not of works; radical, not external; everlasting, not temporary; meetings man's deepest need and transforming his whole being, because from the beginning to the end it would be the work, not of man, but of God himself. In other words, the law which formally was external and accusing now becomes internal, an element of the redeemed nature, and a delight to fulfil.[6]

Contrary to what Neill maintains, both Morris and Hughes most certainly believe that salvation in the Old Testament was essentially the same as in the New. According to Neill, the above writers are suggesting that "the internal operations of divine grace were *not present for the old covenant saint.*"[7] He is essentially saying that both Morris and Hughes deny the blessings of the covenant of grace to Old Testament believers. Nothing, however, could be further from the truth. Morris and Hughes did not say this. They were rather highlighting the difference between believers and non-believers. They were not saying that the blessings of the new covenant only became applicable after the new covenant's formal ratification. They are not alluding to time, but rather to qualitative differences which have always applied to those who embrace the gospel, be it revealed through promise before Christ's incarnation or after his atoning death. For example, in the time of the Mosaic covenant there were those Israelites who knew only the externals—circumcision of the flesh alone, whilst, those Israelites who believed in the promise would have possessed circumcised hearts of flesh, hearts upon which the laws of God were being written. They would have possessed all of this because of the retroactive nature of the new covenant.

Again, R. Scott Clark appears to misunderstand, and obfuscate the 1689 position. One would be justified in asking why? It's not as if what we believe has not, especially in recent years, been clearly

---

6. Neill, "Newness of the New Covenant," 134, quoted from Philip E. Hughes. *A Commentary on the Epistle to the Hebrews*, 300.

7. Neill, "Newness of the New Covenant," 134.

Reformed Baptist Covenant Theology

articulated. Clark insists that the Particular Baptists subscribe to the view that believers, before Christ's completed work, were, although being informed about future redemptive blessings, did not participate in them. The following three quotes make this clear:

> I realized more clearly that for some in the PB tradition the types and shadows *witness* to or *reveal* the coming redemption, which the Old Testament believers have only proleptically, i.e., by anticipation but God the Son is not actually present. By contrast, in the Reformed view . . . the Christ and his benefits, the substance of the covenant of grace, are *in, with,* and *under* the types and shadows. For the PBs Christ and the covenant of grace cannot be in, with, and under the types because, *a priori,* that could only be true in the New Covenant. For the PBs, there is one covenant of grace with one administration: the New Covenant.
>
> For the Reformed, the covenant of grace was in, with, and under the types and shadows. It was not merely a future (New Covenant) reality but it was a present reality, albeit in types and shadows. Thus, when we say "communicated" we mean rather more than the transmission of information. The virtue, benefit, and efficacy was shared to the Old Testament saints by the mysterious operation of the Holy Spirit through the divinely ordained means of grace. How do we know this? From God's Word.
>
> When the Particular Baptists speak of the benefit of Christ being communicated, it seems as if they mean that a future reality was revealed to the Old Testament saints, which they anticipated but which was not actually present for them.[8]

It seems to me that Clark is attempting to understand the Baptist position using Presbyterian categories, in other words, he is experiencing difficulty in setting aside his Presbyterian bias. According to his understanding, the new covenant, being the last

---

8. Clark R. Scott, *One Important Difference Between The Reformed And Some Particular Baptists: God The Son Was In, With, And Under The Types And Shadows.*

The New Covenant in the Old Testament

administration of the one covenant of grace, lay in the future for Old Testament believers, not only in its ratification but in its efficacy. He says that we "conclude that [OT saints like David] did not actually participate in the covenant of grace."

Clark is effectively presenting a caricature of our position. Of course we believe the covenant of grace existed in the Old Testament, only we do not consider it to be the old covenant. Instead, we believe it existed in the promise of the new covenant, with the new covenant being itself the only covenant of grace. By embracing the promise in faith believers who lived before Christ's incarnation became recipients of Christ's future work. To quote Nehemiah Coxe:

> During the time of the law . . . [t]he children of the Lord after the Spirit (though as underage children they were subject to the pedagogy of the law, yet) as to their spiritual and eternal state, walked with God and found acceptance with him on terms of the covenant of grace . . . this spiritual relationship to God [was] according to the terms of the new covenant which the truly godly then had . . .[9]

That efficacy which we accord to the new covenant alone, Clark attaches to the old covenant's "types and shadows". In my view, he confuses these with the antitype. The entire point of the "types and shadows" was to lead men to faith in the antitype—the new covenant in Christ. In themselves, the "types and shadows" were completely useless.

In the first of the above quotes, Clark even implies that we deny Christ's presence to Old Testament believers. He clearly does not appreciate the essential fact that we believe all believers prior to Christ's first coming were in union with the living Christ because the benefits of the new covenant were applied retroactively. Contrary to Clark's misplaced assertions, we believe the benefits of the new covenant were for *all* Old Testament believers a *present*, and not just, as Clark maintains, "a future reality."

The following quote is taken from Clark's article entitled: *Did the Covenant of Grace Begin In The New Covenant?* This title itself

---

9. Coxe, *A Discourse of the Covenants*, 133.

Reformed Baptist Covenant Theology

is somewhat misleading, especially if one is thinking about the formal, legal ratification of the new covenant. Reformed Baptists actually believe that the new covenant is the covenant of grace, i.e., *there is no covenant of grace apart from the new covenant.* This grace has been revealed to sinners since the giving of the first promise in Genesis 3:15. So prior to the new covenant's ratification it existed, not as a formal covenant as such, but as a promise. Other covenants can only be considered "covenants of grace" in so far as they reveal the promise, a promise that speaks of the new covenant in Christ.

According to Clark:

> Adam, Noah, Abraham, and David were all administrations of the covenant of grace. The Scriptures themselves will not allow us to turn Abraham into a covenant of works. Genesis 15:6 is basic to the biblical doctrine of salvation: "Abraham believed God and his faith was credited to him for righteousness." Paul makes much of this by arguing, in Romans 4, that Abraham was the first Christian. He was a Christian when he was a Gentile, before he was circumcised, and he was a Christian after he was circumcised. He is the father of all Christians, Jewish and Gentile alike. Noah found grace in the eyes of Yahweh (Gen 6:8). According to Hebrews 11 Abraham was not looking for land but for heaven. He already believed in the resurrection. That is why he took Isaac up the hill to be sacrificed. Moses identified with Christ rather than Egypt. Who can read the Psalms of David and conclude that he did not actually participate in the covenant of grace but was merely anticipating the New Covenant? Time after time, Noah, Abraham, Moses, and David are portrayed not merely as *anticipating* a future covenant of grace to be inaugurated in the New Covenant, but to be participants in shadowy administrations of the covenant of grace.[10]

Contrary to what Clark might think, this quote is exactly what Reformed Baptists believe. We do not turn the covenant made with Abraham in Genesis 15 into a covenant of works, but, as we shall

---

10. Scott Clark, *Did the Covenant of Grace begin in the New Covenant?*

see later, distinguish between the promise of the new covenant in chapter 15, and the covenant of circumcision in Genesis 17. So in regard to Abraham, we have the ratification of the promise which guarantees the future establishment of the new covenant, and the establishment of the conditional covenant of circumcision, i.e., a covenant revealed by promise and a covenant established. All new covenant blessings belonged to the saints of old because of their faith in the promise. Far from merely anticipating a future new covenant, they encountered the living Christ and participated in the very blessings procured by Christ.

The 1689 Second London Baptist Confession of Faith[11] states:

> Although the price of redemption was not actually paid by Christ till after his incarnation, yet the virtue, efficacy, and benefit thereof were communicated to the elect in all ages, successively from the beginning of the world, in and by those promises, types, and sacrifices wherein he was revealed, and signified to be the seed which should bruise the serpent's head; and the Lamb slain from the foundation of the world, being the same yesterday, and to-day and for ever.[12]

By "virtue, efficacy, and benefit," the Confession simply means that the blessings which Christ's redemptive work would procure were actually "communicated" to all those who believed the promise before the covenant itself was "solemnly sealed, ratified, and confirmed."[13] It most certainly does not mean that such believers merely anticipated the blessings from afar, but, rather, that they experienced them. The "promises, types and sacrifices" of the old covenant served to reveal and signify or signpost the promised seed of Abraham, to engender faith in the Christ, the mediator of the new covenant, the only covenant in which salvation is to be found. Let us then examine what various writers have said concerning this.

Baptist, Greg Nichols, in his book entitled *Covenant Theology*, speaking of salvation under the Mosaic economy states:

11. The First London Baptist Confession was in 1644.
12. 1689 Baptist Confession of Faith 8:6.
13. Owen, *Works*, vol. 22, 64.

Reformed Baptist Covenant Theology

> If the Mosaic covenant cannot regenerate or forgive sinners, how then were sinners saved under its auspices? They had the promise of the Saviour and Messiah (Gen. 3:15, 22:18). They had throughout their history ongoing disclosure of the gospel with ever increasing light and fullness. They had in their religious service many pictures of Christ and his work. The Holy Spirit blessed these gospel promises and pictures of Christ as means of grace. Through them he fulfilled the covenant of grace and created spiritual children of Eve and Abraham. Through those means he regenerated and circumcised their hearts. Thus he blessed Hebrew believers with the spiritual blessings of the new covenant. They had the law written on their hearts, knew the Lord, and had their sins forgiven on the ground of Christ's coming atonement.[14]

John Frame is a Presbyterian, yet he clearly understands the applicability of the new covenant to Old Testament saints:

> [T]he work of Christ is the source of all human salvation from sin: the salvation of Adam and Eve, of Noah, of Abraham, of Moses, of David, and all of God's people in every age, past, present, or future. Everyone who has ever been saved has been saved through the new covenant in Christ. Everyone who is saved receives a new heart of obedience, through the new covenant work of Christ. So though it is the new covenant, it is also the oldest, the temporal expression of the pactum salutis . . . The New Covenant does have a temporal inauguration . . . the shedding of Jesus' blood, a datable historical event, in the substance of the New Covenant, the Covenant that purifies, not only the flesh, but the conscience, the heart. **Nevertheless, as we saw earlier, the efficacy of the New Covenant, unlike that of previous covenants, extends to God's elect prior to Jesus' atonement. When believers in the Old Testament experienced "circumcision of the heart," or when they were Jews "inwardly," they were partaking of the power of the New Covenant.**[15]

---

14. Nichols, *Covenant Theology*, 243. (Bold print added by author)
15. Frame, John, *Systematic Theology*, 79–80.

The New Covenant in the Old Testament

Andrew Woolsey, again a Presbyterian, when examining Augustine of Hippo's understanding of covenant theology informs us that:

> Those who were righteous in the time of the law were also under grace. Christ was their mediator too. Though his incarnation had not yet happened, the fruits of it still availed for all the fathers. Christ was their head . . . So the men of God in the Old Testament were shown to be heirs of the new. *The new covenant was actually more ancient than the old, though it was subsequently revealed. It was 'hidden in the prophetic ciphers' until the time of revelation Also, it was through the operation of the same Holy Spirit that the men of old belonged to "the grace of the new covenant".* So while there were different manifestations in the covenant corresponding to different ages, there was but one testamentum aeternum throughout all ages, entered by faith alone. In every age, everyone, whether children or "decrepit" old men, said Augustine, must come into the new covenant by the regeneration of the Holy Spirit. Only by receiving the Holy Spirit, and not by any power of the human will, could any delight in, or love for, God arise in the soul and begin a movement towards perfection.[16]

It is vital to grasp the essential fact that the "new covenant was actually more ancient than the Old," and that, in Frame's words, "everyone who has ever been saved has been saved through the new covenant in Christ," and that "when believers in the Old Testament experienced 'circumcision of the heart,' or when they were Jews 'inwardly,' they were partaking of the power of the New Covenant."

The prolific 13th century theologian, Thomas Aquinas, clearly understood that there is no salvation for any outside the new covenant:

> The Old Law, which was given to men who were imperfect, that is, who had not yet received spiritual grace, was called the "law of fear," inasmuch as it induced men to observe its commandments by threatening them with

---

16. Woolsey, "The Covenant in the Church Fathers," 42–43. (Italics added for emphasis).

penalties; and is spoken of as containing temporal promises . . . the New Law which derives its pre-eminence from the spiritual grace instilled into our hearts, is called the "Law of love": and it is described as containing spiritual and eternal promises . . . although the Old Law contained precepts of charity, nevertheless it did not confer the Holy Ghost . . . the New Law is chiefly the grace itself of the Holy Ghost, which is given to those who believe in Christ . . . Nevertheless there were some in the state of the Old Testament who, having charity and the grace of the Holy Ghost, looked chiefly to spiritual and eternal promises: and in this respect they belonged to the New Law . . . As to those under the Old Testament who through faith were acceptable to God, in this respect they belonged to the New Testament: for they were not justified except through faith in Christ, Who is the Author of the New Testament . . . *No man ever had the grace of the Holy Ghost except through faith in Christ either explicit or implicit: and by faith in Christ man belongs to the New Testament. Consequently whoever had the law of grace instilled into them belonged to the New Testament . . . at all times there have been some persons belonging to the New Testament, as stated above.*[17]

Some might object to the contention that the new covenant, in terms of its applicability, was before the old covenant, appealing to Jeremiah 31:31, where we read of the new covenant being "after those days." These words are unmistakably speaking of something futuristic. Many, therefore, conclude that the blessings alluded to are only for future believers. This, however, would be a mistake, I say this because the passage is not speaking about the new covenant's applicability, but about its ratification. John Owen anticipated this objection:

> *First*, 'This covenant is promised as that which is *future*, to be brought in at a certain time, "after those days," as has been declared. But it is certain that the things mentioned, the grace and mercy expressed, were really communicated unto many both before and after the giving

17. Aquinas, *Summa Theologica* 1–11, 106–7 (Italics added for emphasis).

The New Covenant in the Old Testament

> of the law, long ere this covenant was made; for all who truly believed and feared God had these things affected in them by grace: wherefore their effectual communication cannot be esteemed a property of this covenant which was afterward made.
>
> *Ans.* This objection was sufficiently prevented in what we have already discoursed concerning the efficacy of the grace of this covenant before it was solemnly consummated. For all things of this nature that belong to unto it do arise and spring from the mediation of Christ, or his interposition on behalf of sinners. Wherefore this took place from the giving of the first promise; the administration of the grace of this covenant did therein and their take its date. Howbeit the Lord Christ had not yet done that whereby it was solemnly to be confirmed, and that whereon all the virtue of it did depend.[18]

Owen is unambiguously saying that the blessings of the new covenant were retroactively applied to believers from the giving of the first promise in Genesis 3:15, even though Christ's redemptive work had not been played out in time. The mediator of the old covenant was Moses, however, the only covenant of which Christ is mediator, where he interposes on behalf of sinners, is the new covenant. Hence, there can be no salvation outside of this covenant.

Calvin is somewhat ambiguous about Old Testament believers being in the new covenant, although in a number of places he suggests they were. Concerning Hebrews 8:10, he writes:

> It may be asked if there was no sure and effective promise of salvation under the Law, if the fathers lacked the grace of the Spirit, if they have no trace of the fatherly favour of God in the remission of their sins? It is evident that they worship God with sincere hearts and pure consciences, and walk in His commandments. This could not have been, unless they had been inwardly taught by the Spirit It is evident that whatever they thought of their sins they were raised up again by their trust in free pardon. Yet the apostle seems to deprive them of both these blessings by referring to the prophecy of Jeremiah to the coming of

---

18. Owen, *Works*, 22, 147.

Reformed Baptist Covenant Theology

> Christ. My answer is that he is not simply denying that God once wrote the Law in their heart and pardoned their sins, but that he is making a comparison between the greater and the less. Because the Father has released the power of His Spirit much more abundantly in the reign of Christ, and has likewise poured out His mercy on mankind, this prominence brings it about that the small portion of grace which He bestowed on the fathers under the Law becomes of no account.[19]

Initially he claims that the new covenant blessings are not for the new covenant alone, but are, comparatively speaking, simply more abundant for those under the new covenant. It's just a matter of new covenant believers having more of what old covenant members had. Ironically, having said this he is forced to acknowledge "the true solution to the question":

> Moreover whatever spiritual gifts the fathers obtained were accidental to the age. It was necessary for them to direct their eyes to Christ to become partakers of them. It is therefore not unreasonable for the apostle in comparing the Gospel with the Law to take away from the latter what is the property of the former. *At the same time there is no reason for God not extending the grace of the new covenant to the fathers. This is the true explanation.*[20]

Again, in his examination of the differences between the Old and New Testaments, or covenants, he states that all believers since the beginning have been in the new covenant:

> The three latter comparisons to which we have referred are of the law and the gospel. In them the law is signified by the name "Old Testament," the gospel by the "New Testament." The first extends more widely, for it includes within itself also the promises published before the law. Augustine, however, said that these should not be reckoned under the name "Old Testament," This was very sensible. He meant the same thing as we are teaching: for he was referring to those statements of Jeremiah and

---

19. Calvin, John. *Hebrews and 1 and 2 Peter*, 112.
20. Calvin, Hebrews and 1 and 2 Peter, 112 (italics added for emphasis)

The New Covenant in the Old Testament

> Paul wherein the Old Testament is distinguished from the word of grace and mercy. *In the same passage he very aptly adds the following: the children of promise [Rom. 9:8], reborn of God, who have obeyed the commands by faith working through love [Gal. 5–6], have belonged to the New Covenant since the world began.* <u>This they did, not in hope of carnal</u>, earthly, and temporal things, but in hope of spiritual, heavenly, and eternal benefits. For they believed especially in the Mediator; and they did not doubt that through him the Spirit was given to them that they might do good, and that they were pardoned whenever they sinned. It is that very point which I intended to affirm: *all the saints whom Scripture mentions as being peculiarly chosen of God from the beginning of the world have shared with us the same blessings of eternal salvation* . . . We must note this about the holy patriarchs: they so lived under the Old Covenant as not to remain there but ever to aspire to the New, and thus embraced a real share in it.[21]

By the "Old Testament" Calvin means the old covenant, this is why he agrees with Augustine when he says that the term "Old Testament" should not be employed to cover the period prior to the giving of the law. It is true, however, that in spite of his acknowledgement of the new covenants retrogressive nature, he continued to believe that the old covenant was a dispensation of the covenant of grace, with both the old and new covenants being of the same substance.[22] In his commentary on Hebrews, Calvin states that any comparisons between the old and new covenants are between "the greater and the less,"[23] that when the prophets speak of the new covenant they are essentially speaking of a greater abundance of what was provided under the old covenant, "Because the Father has released the power of His Spirit much more abundantly in the reign of Christ, and has likewise poured out His mercy on mankind, this prominence brings it about that the small portion of

---

21. Calvin, *Institutes*, 2. 11. 10. (italics for emphasis).
22. Calvin, *Institutes*, 2.10.2.
23. Calvin, *Hebrews* and 1 and 2 Peter 112.

grace which He bestowed on the fathers under the law becomes of no account."[24]

Before concluding this chapter let us look briefly at two important passages from the Old Testament, namely Jeremiah 31:33 and Ezekiel 36:25-28, to examine how the blessings referred to were applied to the believers under the old covenant.

> For this is the covenant that I will make with the house of Israel after those days, declares the Lord: I will put my law within them, and I will write it on their hearts. And I will be their God, and they shall be my people. (Jere 31:33)

> I will sprinkle clean water on you, and you shall be clean from all your uncleannesses, and from all your idols I will cleanse you. And I will give you a new heart, and a new spirit I will put within you. And I will remove the heart of stone from your flesh and give you a heart of flesh. And I will put my Spirit within you, and cause you to walk in my statutes and be careful to obey my rules. You shall dwell in the land that I gave to your fathers, and you shall be my people, and I will be your God. (Ezek 36:25-28)

I said earlier that it was texts like these which caused me considerable vexation in my endeavors to understand covenant theology. The writer to the Hebrews specifically speaks of the Jeremiah passage as being realized in the new covenant (Heb 8:8-13). Presbyterians tell us that the new covenant did not become operative until after its establishment in Christ's shed blood. How, one may ask, if this is the case did believers who lived before the new covenant experience this blessings? This, it seems to me, is a real problem for Presbyterians and they have spilt much ink in their attempts to overcome it. Because of their insistence that the old covenant is an administration of the covenant of grace, they, without Scriptural warrant, and even in defiance of Scripture, make Jesus the mediator of the old covenant.

---

24. Calvin, *Hebrews* and 1 and 2 Peter 112.

The New Covenant in the Old Testament

Scripture makes it plain that Jesus is the mediator only of the new covenant, that "Christ has obtained a ministry that is as much more excellent than the old as the covenant he mediates is better, since it is enacted on better promises" (Heb 8:6). These "better promises," as the writer goes on to say, are those referred to in Jeremiah 31. If they were available under the old covenant they would clearly not be "better." Jesus "is the mediator of a new covenant, so that those who are called may receive the promised eternal inheritance, since a death has occurred that redeems them from the transgressions committed under the first covenant." Had Jesus been the mediator of the old covenant then it would have had some efficacy unto the forgiveness of sins, yet it had none. Indeed, the entire purpose of the letter to the Hebrews is to demonstrate the superiority of the new covenant over the old. There is no way one can rationally maintain Jesus to be the mediator of the old covenant, indeed, the superiority of the new covenant arises from the fact that its mediator is Jesus Christ, and that the blood of this covenant is his own (Matt 26:28; Luke 22:20; 1 Cor 11:25; Heb 12:24).

Neill is quite correct when he says:

> To state the matter as simply as possible, the writing of the law of God on the hearts of his people is not new in the new covenant, nor are the internal operations of God's Holy Spirit upon the hearts and minds of his people new in the new covenant.[25]

His error is simply that he fails to appreciate the fact that these blessings are bestowed upon believers under the old covenant because they are in Christ and the new covenant. New covenant blessings did not first begin with the covenant's establishment but with the first promise of its future establishment. Others believe that the blessings in Jeremiah and Ezekiel will find their fulfilment in the age to come, in the post-second coming kingdom.[26] This

---

25. Neill, "The Newness of the New Covenant" in *The Case For Covenant Infant Baptism*, 236. 127–55

26. Pratt, "Infant Baptism in the New Covenant"

then provides some justification for the idea of covenant breakers in the new covenant, as we will see later.

Although the ratification of the only covenant of which Christ is the mediator, and in which men might find salvation, still lay in the future, all who believed the promise became recipients of the blessings procured by Christ. In other words, the new covenant had a backward or retroactive efficacy. This basic principle applies throughout the OT and is not changed when the various other covenants are imposed. Before Christ ratified the covenant in his shed blood, men and women were saved through faith in the promise. Following Christ's completed work one is saved through faith in the promise's fulfillment. The former look forward to Christ whilst the latter look back to Christ. All Old Testament believers, through faith in the promise, were united to Christ, and they possessed the same redemptive blessings as New Testament believers, i.e., regeneration, justification etc. As we shall see later, if there was one blessing they lacked it was the Spirit of adoption which is a subjective experience whereby the believer is made aware of his position in Christ.

So there we have it. There is no ambiguity about our position. One must not allow the various Old Testament covenants to obfuscate the essential fact that "no man was ever saved but by virtue of the new covenant, and the mediation of Christ therein."[27]

---

27. Owen, *Hebrews*, 22, 70.

5

Application of New Covenant Before Abraham

THE SCRIPTURES ONLY REFER to a handful of believers from the time before the catastrophic flood which destroyed all but Noah and his family, a sum of eight individuals. There were, no doubt, thousands of others that we are not told about who lived and thrived during the pre-flood period, although by Noah's time faith had virtually died out. The few who are spoken about are to teach us that God's salvation in the Old Testament has always been through faith in the promise.

God, in the midst of his pronouncement of the curse for Adam's sin, makes known something of his own plan for dealing with sin (Gen 3:15). He speaks of his placing enmity between the offspring of Eve and the devil: "I will put between you and the woman, and between her offspring and your offspring; he shall bruise your head, and you shall bruise his heel." This is known as the *protoevangelium*, which is the first mention of the approaching gospel or good news. This first promise:

> Implied that God, instead of appearing *against* them as their enemy, was to interpose *for* them as their friend; that He had formed a purpose of grace and mercy towards them, and had devised a plan for their relief and restoration. It implied that, with a view to their ultimate

deliverance, they were to be spared, and placed under a dispensation of forbearance, during which the execution of His penal sentence should be suspended; for their 'seed' is distinctly mentioned, intimating that their lives were to be prolonged[1]

Although the information provided was limited, the *protoevangelion* "contained enough to lay a solid foundation for faith and hope toward God, and it was the first glimmer of Gospel light which dawned on our fallen world."[2] It was not long before men began to call upon the name of the Lord (Gen 4:25), and all who embraced this "first beam of Gospel light" in faith were saved in exactly the same way as are believers today, only they believed God's promise while we look to the promise's fulfilment. To sum up, the promise

> ... implied that the 'woman's Seed'-the promised deliverer- was now to be the Hope of the world, and the Head of a redeemed people, who should be rescued from the curse of the Law, and restored to the favour and friendship of God; for Adam, the head of the old covenant, is superseded under the new, by One who is predicated and promised as 'the Seed of the woman.' It implied an 'election according to grace,' for distinct mention is made of 'the woman's seed,' and 'the serpent's seed;' and the serpent's seed are left under the curse, while the woman's seed are delivered from it.[3]

While the new covenant would not be formally established until Christ came, all who believed the promise would, nevertheless, have had the blessings procured by the mediator of this covenant applied retroactively to them.

The Apostle tells us that "sin indeed was in the world before the law was given, but sin is not counted where there is no law. Yet death reigned from Adam to Moses ..." (Rom 5:13-14). In other words, because death was present, and "the wages of sin is death"

---

1. Buchanan, *The Doctrine of Justification*, 26.
2. Buchanan, *The Doctrine of Justification*, 27.
3. Buchanan, *The Doctrine of Justification*, 27.

Application of New Covenant Before Abraham

(Rom 6:23) there must have been a law present. Even though the law was not written, as it would later be, on tablets of stone, the works of God's law is written upon the hearts of all men (Rom 2:15). From the creation, all are aware of the law and are without excuse. It was against this backdrop that the promises of God shined forth. The law could now only pronounce condemnation, whereas the promise spoke of salvation in the seed of the woman.

The shadows of the Old Testament have made way for the clear light of day in the New Testament, and, consequently, we should always view the Old through the lens of the New. We are told that "faith is the assurance of things hoped for, the conviction of things not seen", and that it was by faith "the people of old received their commendation" (Heb 11:2). Abel's bloody offering was accepted by God because it spoke about the future offering of Christ, although Abel would have seen through a very dark glass. He offered in faith a sacrifice which was accepted by God, while that of his brother, Cain, was rejected.

> Now Abel was a keeper of sheep, and Cain a worker of the ground. In the course of time Cain brought to the Lord an offering of the fruit of the ground, and Abel also brought of the firstborn of his flock and of their fat portions. And the Lord had regard for Abel and his offering, but for Cain and his offering he had no regard. So Cain was very angry, and his face fell. (Gen. 4:2–5).

It was not because of his offering that he was accepted by the Lord, but the Lord accepted his offering because he was already justified. Abel may not have possessed the knowledge of exactly what had occurred to him, he did, however, know acceptance with his God. He would have been regenerated by the Holy Spirit, his heart of stone would have been replaced by one of flesh and he was a new man in Jesus Christ. His gift was essentially an expression of his faith; a declarative justification by faith. It was this that distinguished him from his brother Cain, "By faith Abel offered to God a more acceptable sacrifice than Cain, through which he was commended as righteous, God commending him by accepting his gifts" (Heb 11:4). As John Gill puts it:

> His sacrifice was a more excellent one; not only as to its king, being a lamb, and so typical of the Lamb of God; but as to the manner in which it was offered, by faith, in view of a better sacrifice than that; even the sacrifice of Christ, by which transgression is finished, sin made an end of, reconciliation for it made, and an everlasting righteousness brought in; all which Abel, by faith, looked unto, and God had respect to him, and to his offering.[4]

Mention needs to be made of Enoch. We are told that he "walked with God, and he was not, for God took him" (Gen 5:24). The writer to the Hebrews says that "Enoch was taken up so that he should not see death, and he was not found, because God had taken him. Now before he was taken he was commended as having pleased God" (Heb 11:5). As with Abel, Enoch pleased God because he had faith in what God had promised, for we know that (without faith it is impossible to please him, for whoever would draw near to God must believe that he exists and that he rewards those who seek him" (Heb 11:6).

Noah is perhaps the most prominent of the characters spoken about who lived in those antediluvian times. We are told that in Noah's day "the LORD saw that wickedness of man was great in the earth, and that every intention of the thoughts of his heart was only evil continually" (Gen 6:5). Noah was unique in those days in that he "found favour in the eyes of the Lord," being "a righteous man, blameless in his generation. Noah walked with God"(Gen 6:8–9), and was a "preacher of righteousness" (2 Pet 2:5 KJV). The very righteousness he so faithfully declared was the same righteousness by which he himself was declared justified before God; it was the righteousness of Christ imputed. With the impending flood, Noah would have warned the people, calling upon them to renounce sin and put their faith in God's promises. "By faith, Noah, being warned by God concerning events as yet unseen, in reverent fear constructed an ark for saving his household. By this he condemned the world and became an heir of the righteousness that comes by faith" (Heb 11:7). The "spirits in prison" whom Peter

---

4. Gill, *Body of Divinity*, vol.1, 496.

Application of New Covenant Before Abraham

refers to were the lost souls to whom Noah declared the gospel, and who refused to believe.

With Noah we have a transition from the old world that was destroyed in the deluge to a new beginning from Noah's family. God tells Noah that he will establish his covenant with him (Gen 6:18). This is the first mention of the covenant (*berith*) in Scripture. While this covenant is not directly pointing to the new covenant in Christ, it does guarantee God's common grace for mankind; preserving humanity for the outworking of God's salvific purposes. In other words, it served to vouchsafe the necessary environment for the application of salvation through time. To quote Gill:

> The covenant made with Noah, though it was not the special covenant of grace, being made with him and all his posterity, and even with all creatures; yet as it was a covenant of preservation, it was a covenant of kindness and goodness in a temporal way; and it bore a resemblance to the covenant of grace; inasmuch as there were no conditions in it, no sign or token to be observed on man's part: only what God himself gave as a token of his good will, the rainbow in the cloud; and seeing that it was a covenant, durable, lasting, and inviolable.[5]

The first promise in Genesis 3:15 continued through Noah's son, Shem. We see in this covenant the establishment of the covenantal promise that would be progressively revealed in greater fulness and clarity until reaching its telos in the establishment of the new covenant in Christ. And, although this lay in the distant future, all who believed would have shared in Christ's future work because of the new covenants retroactive efficacy.

---

5. Gill, *Body of Divinity*, vol.1, 499.

6

Promissory Covenant with Abraham

Disagreement between the Presbyterians/Baptists can be traced back to our different understanding of the Abrahamic covenant. As we shall see, while the former believe that only one covenant was established with Abraham, the Reformed Baptists distinguish between the covenant established with Abraham, what is essentially the old covenant, and the new covenant which was revealed to him in the promise.

With Abraham we have a major advancement made in the application of God's redemptive purposes. In the words of Golding:

> it marks a completely new phase in the divine purpose for mankind. Until this point in history, God had dealt with the human race more or less as a whole. Individuals such as Abel, Enoch and Noah had been singled out of special blessing, but the faithful were scattered among many branches of the human family. But, with the Abrahamic covenant, there is a narrowing-down process, and the divine redemptive purpose is channeled into one particular branch of Noah's family tree, the line that descends through Shem and Terah to Abraham, of whom Christ is born.[1]

---

1. Golding, *Covenant Theology*, 154.

Promissory Covenant with Abraham

In examining God's dealings with Abraham, it is essential to distinguish between the promise that was revealed to him in Genesis chapters 12 and 15, and the covenant that was established with him in chapter 17. The promise was first revealed to him in Genesis 12:1–3, where we read:

> Now the Lord said to Abram, "Go from your country and your kindred and your father's house to the land that I will show you. And I will make of you a great nation, and I will bless you and make your name great, so that you will be a blessing. I will bless those who bless you, and him who dishonors you I will curse, and in you all the families of the earth shall be blessed."

It is important to note that these words were spoken to Abraham, or Abram, as he was then known, some years before the covenant of circumcision.

The Jews took great pride in the fact that they were Abraham's physical offspring; that they were the people of the circumcision etc. The Apostle, however, circumvented their boasting by showing that the Patriarch's true spiritual children can trace their ancestry, not to the later covenant of circumcision, but to Abraham's faith in the promised gospel some twenty-five years before (Gal 3:17).

About this promise, Nehemiah Coxe states:

> The sum of all gospel blessings is comprised in this promise. Therefore, it will follow that the proper heirs of this blessing of Abraham have a right (not only in some, but) in all the promises of the new covenant. This is not true in a limited sense, suspended on uncertain conditions, but in the full sense and secured by the infinite grace, wisdom, power, and faithfulness of God.[2]

The gospel that was preached to Abraham was nothing less than the good news about Christ and the future new covenant. as Coxe states:

> the sum and substance of all spiritual and eternal blessings was included in the covenant and promise given to

---

2. Coxe, *A Discourse of the Covenants*, 81.

Reformed Baptist Covenant Theology

Abraham (Genesis 12) in these words: "I will bless you, and you will be a blessing." The grace and blessings of the new covenant were given and ensured to Abraham for himself. What is more, this honor was conferred on him that he should be a head of covenant blessings as the father of all true believers.[3]

Whilst Coxe speaks of the covenant in chapter 12, the word (*berith*) is not actually referred to until Genesis 15, where we see the establishment of a 'promissory covenant.' It is probable, therefore, that the promises found in chapter 12 are ratified in this chapter.

Presbyterians maintain that the covenant referred to in Genesis 15 is essentially the same covenant of grace as in chapter 17.[4] They then maintain that there was only one covenant with Abraham and this was a covenant of grace. When Paul says that the law which was given 430 years after the promise does not abrogate or in any way change a previous covenant so as to make the promise of no effect (Gal 3:17), he is, we are told, alluding to the covenant established in Genesis 17, which itself encompasses any previous references to the covenant. So, essentially, the text is saying that the law did not set aside or change the covenant of grace established with Abraham in Genesis 17. This is in contrast to the Baptist position which distinguishes between the revelation of the new covenant in Genesis 15 and the establishment of what is a conditional covenant of works in chapter 17.

In his letter to the Galatians Paul was combatting opponents who were saying that to be truly saved it was necessary for the believer to submit to circumcision; a rite which they considered part of the law or old covenant.[5] This being the case, it is most unlikely that, in opposing circumcision, Paul would have been considering Genesis 17 in his reference to the covenant and promise in

---

3. Coxe, *A Discourse of the Covenants*, 75.

4. This is also the view of many Baptists. For example, Jeffrey Johnson, in *The Fatal Flaw*, maintains that Genesis chapters 15 and 17 are referring to one and the same covenant, and that this covenant is to be untangled to determine its conditional and unconditional aspects.

5. Although the law came through Moses over 430 years after the rite.

Promissory Covenant with Abraham

Galatians 3:17. This is because he would essentially be playing into the hands of the Judaizers. They would be able to respond, saying that the promise was dependent on the rite of circumcision, after all, circumcision was the essential condition for this covenant. The only way to circumvent his opponents is for Paul to refer to a covenant promise that was given before the institution of the rite. He does this by alluding to Genesis 15. Here the promise itself was guaranteed by a promissory covenant. This being the case, nothing that came afterwards, e.g., circumcision, the Mosaic law, could abrogate or change the promise.

Paul does the same thing in Romans chapter 4:9–16. Having been one himself, he understood the way the Judaizers thought. He knew the arguments they would use. For them, observance of the law and circumcision were considered prerequisites for salvation. As in Galatians, the Apostle demonstrates that God's salvific blessing was given to Abraham prior to circumcision (Rom 4:9–11). He again does this by harkening back to Genesis 15, showing that Abraham was credited with righteousness, justified by faith alone, before the rite was instituted (Gen 15:5).

In Genesis 15 we essentially have a covenant promising a covenant. In this context the covenant consists of a "commitment certified by an oath."[6] God is promising the new covenant, the formal establishment of which lay nearly two thousand years in the future. This is the very same covenant spoken of by Paul (Gal 3:17). It is, in the words of John Gill:

> 'a covenant confirmed of God in Christ', a covenant in which Christ is concerned; a covenant made with him, of which he is the sum and substance, the Mediator, surety, and messenger; and such is what the Scriptures call the covenant of life and peace, and what we commonly style the covenant of grace and redemption; because the articles of redemption and reconciliation, of eternal life and salvation, by the free grace of God, are the principal things in it.[7]

---

6. Waldron, *A Modern Exposition of the 1689 Baptist Confession*, 117.

7. Gill, *Genesis 15*, Biblestudytools.com

Abraham is promised a son, although he was well advanced in years (v.4), and that his offspring would number the stars in the heavens (v.5). This is the promise he believed and by which he was justified before God (although it is likely that this was a reaffirmation of the justification he received after believing the first promise in chapter 12:2–3). It is to this oath that the writer to the Hebrews makes reference to:

> For when God made a promise to Abraham, since he had no one greater by whom to swear, he swore by himself, saying, "Surely I will bless you and multiply you." And thus Abraham, having patiently waited, obtained the promise. For people swear by something greater than themselves, and in all their disputes an oath is final for confirmation. So when God desired to show more convincingly to the heirs of the promise the unchangeable character of his purpose, he guaranteed it with an oath, so that by two unchangeable things, in which it is impossible for God to lie, we who have fled for refuge might have strong encouragement to hold fast to the hope set before us. (Hebrews 6:13–18)

The Lord also promised Abraham physical land. This temporal blessing would serve as a type of the more important eternal spiritual blessings. As Coxe says:

> It will readily be granted that some of those promises that ultimately respect the spiritual seed and spiritual blessings are sometimes given to Abraham under the cover of those terms that have an immediate respect to his natural seed and temporal blessings as types of the other.[8]

In Genesis 15 there are no stipulations attached to the promises. Abraham is simply a passive receiver. In this regard it is a covenant similar to that made with Noah and his sons, where we read:

> Then God said to Noah and to his sons with him, "Behold, I establish my covenant with you and your offspring after you, and with every living creature that is with you, the birds, the livestock, and every beast of the earth with you,

---

8. Coxe, *A Discourse of the Covenants*, 76.

Promissory Covenant with Abraham

as many as came out of the ark; it is for every beast of the earth. I establish my covenant with you, that never again shall all flesh be cut off by the waters of the flood, and never again shall there be a flood to destroy the earth." (Gen 9:8–11)

Noah simply received that which the Lord promises to do.

God instructed Abraham (Abram) to gather up a selection of wildlife, to slaughter them, and, with the exception of the birds, to cut them in half and lay "each half over against the other" (Gen 15:9–10). Later, after falling into a deep sleep, he witnessed the Lord himself symbolically passing between the dismembered carcases (v.17).

What, one may ask, was the significance of this covenantal inauguration? It seems, in the words of O. Palmer Robertson that

> The animal division symbolizes a "pledge to the death" at the point of covenant commitment. The dismembered animals represent the curse that the covenant-maker calls down on himself if he should violate the commitment which he has made.[9]

We find something similar in Jeremiah 34:18–20:

> And the men who transgressed my covenant and did not keep the terms of the covenant that they made before me, I will make them like the calf that they cut in two and passed between its parts.—the officials of Judah, the officials of Jerusalem, the eunuchs, the priests, and all the people of the land who passed between the parts of the calf. And I will give them into the hand of their enemies and into the hand of those who seek their lives. Their dead bodies shall be food for the birds of the air and the beasts of the earth. "

In other words, the men had broken the conditions of the covenant and were going to suffer the fate of the dismembered animal. The essential difference in Genesis 15 is that it is not the people but the Lord himself who passes between the divided animal parts. It

---

9. O. Palmer Robinson, *The Christ of the Covenants*, 10.

is a unilateral covenant of the Lord with God himself "cutting the covenant." The covenant is said to be ratified, because, as Waldron reminds us, "a covenant is more than a mere promise. It is a sworn promise. It is certified by an oath. It is a promise legally secured by a formal oath."[10]

The significance of this is that the covenantal promises are guaranteed. Of course, God's word alone should be sufficient. It seems that in swearing an oath he is "at pains to assure his people of the utter certainty of his promises, of his faithfulness, of their utter security in his love and grace."[11]

In his letter to the Galatians (3:16–17), concerning the promises made in Genesis 12 and 15, the Apostle says:

> Now the promises were made to Abraham and to his offspring. It does not say, "And to offsprings," referring to many, but referring to one, "And to your offspring," who is Christ. This is what I mean: the law which came 430 years afterward does not annul a covenant previously ratified by God, so as to make the promise void.[12]

One might ask how this can be reconciled with the contention that the only covenant of grace is the new covenant, a covenant that was not ratified until Christ shed his blood. For clearly, in this verse (Gal 3:17) Paul is saying that what we regard as the covenant of grace was ratified 430 years before the law of Moses was given. In calling the covenant in Genesis 15 "ratified," the Apostle is essentially speaking not of the new covenant in itself, the thing promised, but, rather, the ratification of the promise. The Lord is guaranteeing the future establishment of the new covenant in Christ. Imagine that I promise my son that next year I will purchase for him a new car. To this end I swear an oath. My son knows

---

10. Waldron, *A Modern Exposition of the 1689 Baptist Confession of Faith*, 117.

11. Waldron, *A Modern Exposition of the 1689 Baptist Confession of Faith*, 117.

12. The ESV Bible translates the Greek as "offspring" and "offsprings", In what follows I will often use the King James Bible which translates the word as "seed" and "seeds".

Promissory Covenant with Abraham

me and knows that I always do what I promise. When next year arrives, I take him to the garage and I buy him the car. The promise is obviously not the same as the actual purchase, although in both instances the covenant can be said to be ratified. On the one hand we have the covenant of promise which is ratified through the oath, and on the other, we have the covenant that is ratified in the actual purchase of the car. In Galatians 3:17, Paul is alluding to the ratification of the promise, knowing that its ratification by God is as good as the actual ratification of the thing promised. For truly, "all the promises of it are ratified as he was the surety of the covenant . . . and in him they are all 'Yes" and 'Amen.'"[13]

Christ, being the fulfilment of the promise, becomes the covenant keeper and the covenant transgressor. In the former he fulfilled all the conditions of the original covenant of works, and in the latter, he received in his own body the consequences of the covenant breaker. In the words of Ray Vander Laan:

> When God made covenant with his people. He did something no human being would have even considered doing. In the usual blood covenant, each party was responsible for keeping only his side of the promise. When God made covenant with Abraham, however, he promised to keep *both* sides of the agreement.
>
> "If this covenant is broken, Abraham, for whatever reason-for My unfaithfulness or yours-I will pay the price," said God. "If you or your descendants, for whom you are making this covenant, fail to keep it, I will pay the price in blood."
>
> At that moment, Almighty God pronounced the death sentence on his Son Jesus.[14]

The promises made to Abraham, as well as speaking of the future new covenant in Christ, as mentioned earlier, also speak of the land. In chapter 15 Abraham is promised the land unconditionally (v.7; 18ff). This unconditional initial giving of the land here serves

---

13. Coxe, *A Discourse of the Covenants*, 76.

14. Ray Vander Laan with Judith Markham, *Echoes of His Presence: Stories of the Messiah from the People of His Day*, 9

as a type of the unconditional spiritual promises referred to in Gen 12:1–3 and 15:2–6. The land also serves as a token of the Lord's faithfulness in keeping what he has promised. As we shall see later, this did not guarantee Israel's continuance in the land. The land always belonged to the Lord (Lev 25:23), and anyone residing there, if they were to continue in the land and reap the blessings, would have to conform to his standards. Israel, however, defiled the land and turned the Lord's heritage into an abomination (Jer 2:7).

7

The Covenant of Circumcision

Prior to God's calling of Abram, the promise first revealed in Gen 3:15 had been universal, i.e., it was not confined to a particular people. With Abraham we see, for the first time, particularization of a people, i.e., Abraham's physical offspring. This occurred because it was through this people the Lord was going to bring the Messiah into the world; the one in whom, and on account of whose work, the spiritual new covenant blessings find their origin.

As we have seen, the covenant made with Abraham in Genesis 17 must not be considered the same as the promissory covenant spoken of in chapter 15. It is not simply another side of the earlier covenant. The covenant revealed in chapter 15 would find its formal establishment and ratification in Abraham's seed (singular)—the Messiah. The covenant in chapter 17, on the other hand, was established and ratified with Abraham and his offspring (plural). This covenant did, however, reiterate the unconditional promises made earlier, although these were couched within the context of the conditional temporal blessings. So while this covenant was conditional and spoke of temporal blessings, it also signposted the promise through which eternal spiritual blessings were available to all who, like Abraham, believed.

Before examining the conditional nature of this covenant I briefly want to look at the meaning of the word "everlasting" as it is applied here. For example, in verse 7 of chapter 17 we read, "And I will give to you and to your offspring after you the land of your sojournings, and all of the land of Canaan, for an everlasting possession, and I will be their God." At first glance one would be forgiven for thinking that "forever" means lasting forever, having no terminus. Closer inspection, however, shows that this is not the case. The Hebrew word is not the same as its English translation; it does not possess the same infinite application. Concerning "everlasting" Christopher Wright tells us:

> When the land, the kings and the priests were declared to be 'forever', it meant that these dimensions were permanent and guaranteed while Israel as a nation was the limit of God's redemptive work and covenant relationship. Once this national and territorial basis was transcended through the coming of the Messiah and the extension of the gospel of redemption to Gentiles and Jews through him, then the 'forever-ness' of these things resides in Christ himself, the embodiment of Israel.[1]

We see examples of this, in, for example, the Aaronic Priesthood (1 Chron 23:13)[2]. It was said to have been forever, but, as we read in Hebrews 8:13, this was far from being the case. In the tabernacle, all the ceremonies were to last "forever" (Ex 27:21), and the Sabbath was to be a sign "forever" (Ex 31:16–17). All of these things, however, came to an end. Whatever then is signified by the word "forever" it clearly does not mean something without end, or infinite.

So what does "everlasting" mean when it is used in the above contexts? Let me quote what John Reisinger says:

> It may mean that something is given as a physical and temporary 'type' of something else that is spiritual and eternal. The thing promised becomes truly everlasting as it finds its fulfilment in its antitype. Israel is a nation before God 'forever' as it is fulfilled in the church, the

---

1. Wright, Christopher, "A Christian Approach to Old Testament Prophecy Concerning Israel," 6.
2. See also Exodus 40:15; Numbers 25:13.

The Covenant of Circumcision

true 'Israel of God.' Aaron is a priest 'forever' as he finds his fulfilment in Christ our High Priest. The Sabbath is a sign forever as it finds its fulfilment in eternal rest in Christ. God's people will indeed dwell secure in the true holy land forever as they eternally rest in Christ.[3]

In Gen 17:8 the land is promised as an "everlasting possession." We shall see, especially when we examine the Mosaic covenant, that this was conditional. The physical land served as a type of the land Abraham saw in faith (Heb 11:10,16). Israel's continued possession of the physical land, the type, was predicated on obedience which it was unable to provide. However, the antitype, the spiritual eternal land was guaranteed because, although still conditional, it was guaranteed because the required obedience was provided vicariously by the promised Christ. Where the first man hopelessly failed, the second man would triumphantly succeed.

It may also be that 'everlasting' may denote that something is going to last for the entire duration of the institution it is associated with. Those institutions of the old covenant, for example, the Aaronic priesthood, the various food laws etc., lasted throughout that covenant's duration. When the covenant came to an end, so did the various institutions associated with it.

The condition of the covenant was circumcision, indeed, Scripture refers to it as "the covenant of circumcision" (Acts 7:8), "This is my covenant which you shall keep, between me and you and your offspring after you: Every male among you shall be circumcised" (Gen 17:10). This rite, however, meant much more than the simple surgical removal of the foreskin, "It symbolized full obedience of the law from the heart" (Deut 30:6).[4] As the Apostle reminds us, "For circumcision is indeed of value if you obey the law, but if you break the law, your circumcision becomes uncircumcision" (Rom 2:25), and again, "I testify again to every man who accepts circumcision that he is obligated to keep the whole law" (Gal 5:3).

---

3. Reisinger, *Abraham's Four Seeds*, 89.
4. Johnson, *The Kingdom of God*, 51.

Reformed Baptist Covenant Theology

The great promises given to Abraham in Genesis 17 were conditional upon the obedience of both Abraham and his descendants. Abraham is told to walk before the Lord and be blameless (Gen 17:1). He was commanded to teach his children to do likewise:

> The Lord said, "Shall I hide from Abraham what I am about to do, seeing that Abraham shall surely become a great and mighty nation, and all the nations of the earth shall be blessed in him? For I have chosen him, that he may command his children and his household after him to keep the way of the Lord by doing righteousness and justice, so that the Lord may bring to Abraham what he has promised him." (Gen 18:17–19)

When the Lord renewed the covenant with Isaac, he said to him:

> I will multiply your offspring as the stars of heaven and I will give to your offspring all these lands. And in your offspring all the nations of the world shall be blessed, because Abraham obeyed my voice and kept my charge, my commandments, my statutes, and my laws. (Gen 26:4–5)

Israel was, therefore, under the law before it even reached Sinai. Prior to being provided with manna the Lord told Moses that he was going to test the people to see "whether they will walk in my law or not" (Ex 16:4). Because some of the people gathered the manna on the Sabbath, the Lord responded "How long will you refuse to keep my commandments and my laws" (Ex 16:28). Jeffrey Johnson makes an interesting point concerning this:

> . . . the Mosaic covenant was established with the physical children of Abraham—the same group of people who were placed under the conditions of the Abrahamic covenant. If the Abrahamic covenant had been purely a covenant of grace for the physical seed of Abraham, then it would have been unjust of God to place the same group of people under the Mosaic covenant of works. Therefore, the only way the covenant of works (republished in the Mosaic covenant) could have been established with the physical seed of Abraham was for the physical seed

of Abraham to have already been obligated to obey the moral law of God in the Abrahamic covenant.[5]

Abraham's circumcision was unique because he was the only one to be circumcised after having believed. A seal is only given for something that has already occurred. For Abraham alone was circumcision a seal of the fact that the foreskin of his heart had been cut off, i.e., he was already in possession of what circumcision pointed to. For all others the rite was only a sign signifying that should they walk in Abraham's footsteps; a spiritual circumcision was a possibility.

Reformed paedobaptists believe there to be an exact correspondence between circumcision and baptism, the former has simply been replaced by the latter, yet both speak of the same spiritual realities. By doing this they appear to have distorted any similarities that do exist. Concerning Colossians 2:11–12, Calvin asks:

> What is the meaning of this language, but that of accomplishment and truth of baptism is the same with the accomplishment and truth of circumcision, since they both represent the same thing? For Paul's design is to show that baptism was to the Christian the same as circumcision had before been to the Jews. But as we have now clearly evinced that the promises of these two signs and the mysteries represented are by them precisely the same, we shall insist no longer on this point at present. I will only recommend believers to consider, whether the sign ought to be accounted earthly and literal, which contains nothing but what is spiritual and heavenly.[6]

Circumcision, unlike baptism, as we have seen, possessed a national significance in that it served to mark off Israel from surrounding nations. It was to "serve as a continual reminder that from the Abrahamic stock the promised Seed would spring."[7]

The error paedobaptists make lies in their tendency to neglect this temporal significance of the rite, focusing only on the

---

5. Johnson, *The Kingdom of God*, 62–63.
6. Calvin, *Institutes*, III. XI. 1
7. Pink, *The Divine Covenants*, 97.

spiritual. Yes, circumcision pointed to the possibility of a spiritual circumcision of the heart, however, for all faithless Jews, those who did not follow in Abraham's footsteps by believing, the rite, contrary to Calvin's conclusion, had no spiritual significance at all.

One cannot then simply say that the two rites mean the same thing, for example, according to John Murray:

> Of particular note is the fact that the leading notion in the meaning of circumcision is identical in principle with the leading notion in the meaning of baptism, namely, union and communion with the Lord. And it is of paramount importance to take due account of the fact that it was by divine institution and command that the sign and seal of such blessings was administered to infants in the old economy. Circumcision, signifying what in principle is identical with that signified by baptism, was administered to infants who were born within the covenant relation and privilege.[8]

Murray is correct to call circumcision a sign, but incorrect to call it a seal to any but Abraham. A seal speaks of something that has already taken place, it is a confirmation of authenticity. Circumcision may have been a seal of membership to carnal Israel, but concerning spiritual realities the rite served only as a sign suggesting a future possibility, not a present reality. Baptism can only be compared to the circumcision of the heart, where the possibilities it speaks of have been realized through faith.

Distinguishing between the carnal and spiritual Israel, David Kingdon comments:

> So those who were born after the flesh, although they had an interest in the earthly blessings promised in the covenant, had no interest in the spiritual and eternal inheritance that God declared would be the lot of his people.. They belonged in a physical sense to the seed of Abraham, but they were not the seed of Abraham's faith.[9]

---

8. Murray, *Christian Baptism*, 48.
9. Kingdon, *Children of Abraham*, 32.

The Covenant of Circumcision

Baptism, in contrast, does not speak of possibilities, but of a new life already attained in Christ. The Apostle puts both rites together in Colossians 2:11–12,

> In him also you were circumcised with a circumcision made without hands, by putting off the body of flesh, by the circumcision of Christ, having been buried with him in baptism, in which you were also raised with him through faith in the powerful working of God, who raised him from the dead.

Paul is not referring here to circumcision as it existed for the unsaved Jew, but of circumcision as it applied to those who believed, those who knew circumcision of the heart. This is why he speaks of it being "made without hands," it is the work of God in the heart. Baptism is a rite that speaks of the position of those who have undergone this spiritual circumcision; both rites are then concerned with the same inner reality.

God's true spiritual children consists only of those who exercise faith, only these constitute what Paul calls the "Israel of God" (Gal 6:15,16). While circumcision was administered to all of Abraham's seeds, it was only a remnant who experienced spiritual circumcision. All Jews were circumcised on the eighth day, with a circumcision "made with hands," yet most never knew the circumcision "made without hands." There was never even the assumption of the former implying the latter, except in regard to a future possibility, yet despite this, many Reformed paedobaptists somehow assume that a baptized child is born of the Spirit of God. Baptists, on the other hand, maintain that all who undergo believers' baptism have made a profession of faith, with the rite celebrating a completed circumcision of the heart in Christ, as Sam Waldron puts it, "Baptism, therefore, professes what circumcision demanded. Circumcision did demand a new heart, indeed, but it did not profess a new heart. Baptism professes a new heart."[10]

There are then two levels of meaning in the covenant established with Abraham, what one may call the dispensational and

---

10. Waldron, *A Modern Exposition of the 1689 Confession of Faith*, 351.

trans-dispensational levels, one relating to the type, the other to the antitype. The former speaks to Abraham's physical seed (plural), while the latter relates to his seed (singular) who is the Christ and this includes all those who have faith. On the one level there are the conditional promises which relate to physical Israel, for example, God promises to Abraham the land of Canaan, and that from his offspring will come forth nations, and kings; although the continuation of these are conditional upon the people's obedience. The antitypical level, in contrast, speaks of the eternal realities whose fulfillment is guaranteed on account of the Christ's obedience, the blessings of which are communicated to all, should they, like Abraham, believe the promises.

Let us briefly examine how the types and antitypes play out in regard to the kingship and land promises (Gen 17:6, 8). Kingship, in the temporal typical sense, reached its fulfillment in the Davidic kingship. As we go through the Old Testament we see a narrowing down of the line of descent, from Abraham, through Isaac and Jacob, through Judah until we get to David. The spiritual fulfillment, as we know, is manifested in the Messiah, the Christ. As David lay dying God said to him:

> When your days are fulfilled and you lie down with your fathers, I will raise up your offspring after you, who shall come from your body, and I will establish his kingdom. He shall build a house for my name, and I will establish the throne of his kingdom forever. I will be to him a father, and he shall be to me a son. When he commits iniquity, I will discipline him with the rod of men, with the stripes of the sons of men, but my steadfast love will not depart from him, as I took it from Saul, whom I put away from before you. And your house and your kingdom shall be made sure forever before me. Your throne shall be established forever.'" In accordance with all these words, and in accordance with all this vision, Nathan spoke to David. (2 Samuel 7:13–17)

Some might think that this is a reference to Solomon. Yet his throne did not last forever because of sin. However, one did come forth

The Covenant of Circumcision

from David's offspring whose throne does last forever or eternally. This is the very one Peter speaks of:

> Brothers, I may say to you with confidence about the patriarch David that he both died and was buried, and his tomb is with us to this day. Being therefore a prophet, and knowing that God had sworn with an oath to him that he would set one of his descendants on his throne, he foresaw and spoke about the resurrection of the Christ, that he was not abandoned to Hades, nor did his flesh see corruption. This Jesus God raised up, and of that we all are witnesses. Being therefore exalted at the right hand of God, and having received from the Father the promise of the Holy Spirit, he has poured out this that you yourselves are seeing and hearing. For David did not ascend into the heavens, but he himself says,
>
> > "'The Lord said to my Lord,
> > "Sit at my right hand,
> > until I make your enemies your footstool."'
>
> Let all the house of Israel therefore know for certain that God has made him both Lord and Christ, this Jesus whom you crucified." (Acts 2:29–36)

One can then understand why Matthew opens his gospel with the words, "The book of the genealogy of Jesus Christ, the son of David, the son of Abraham" (Matt 1:1).

In the temporal king David we have the type of the antitype who is Christ. While God fulfilled his promise to give natural Israel a king, continuance of the kingship was impossible because it was dependent on a sinful people's obedience, whereas the spiritual eternal kingship it pointed to was established on the sure and certain foundation of the obedience of God's very own Son.

The physical land plays a prominent part in the covenant. There are literally hundreds of references to the land in the Old Testament. It was one of the chief promises of the old covenant. The Lord is always faithful to his promises and there was never any question as to whether he would give Israel the land. As Joshua 21:43–45 reminds us:

> Thus the Lord gave to Israel all the land that he swore to give to their fathers. And they took possession of it, and they settled there. And the Lord gave them rest on every side just as he had sworn to their fathers. Not one of all their enemies had withstood them, for the Lord had given all their enemies into their hands. Not one word of all the good promises that the Lord had made to the house of Israel had failed; all came to pass.

Continuity in the land is, however, always dependent upon Israel's obedience. Look at what the Lord says in Psalm 105:10–11, where the Psalmist is remembering how the Lord saved Israel from bondage and led her into Canaan:

> He remembers his covenant forever,
> the word that he commanded for a
> thousand generations
> the covenant that he made with Abraham,
> his sworn promise to Isaac
> which he confirmed to Jacob as
> a statute
> to Israel as an everlasting covenant
> saying, "To you I give the
> land of Canaan
> as your portion and inheritance."

as we read in verses 44, 45:

> And he gave them the lands of
> The nations and they took possession of the
> Fruit of the people's toil,
> That they might keep his
> Statutes and observe his laws.

To simply quote the earlier verses would give one the impression that God would give the land without there being conditions that Israel would need to fulfil, but as the latter verses make clear, faithfulness to the Lord's statutes was essential if Israel was to remain in the land.

The physical land did, however, serve to point to another land, one that would be made possible because of Christ's redemption

The Covenant of Circumcision

work. Those of faith did not look forward to some this-worldly *real estate*, as the writer to the Hebrews puts it:

> These all died in faith, not having received the things promised, but having seen them and greeted them from afar, and having acknowledged that they were strangers and exiles on the earth. For people who speak thus make it clear that they are seeking a homeland. If they had been thinking of that land from which they had gone out, they would have had opportunity to return. But as it is, they desire a better country, that is, a heavenly one. Therefore God is not ashamed to be called their God, for he has prepared for them a city. (Hebrews 11:13–16)

The promises of what might have been in the physical realm had Israel kept her side of the covenant would ultimately find their fulfillment in the new covenant, in the new heaven and new earth spoken of by John (Rev 21), made possible because of Christ's substitutionary atonement. Concerning the land promise in Genesis 17:8, Anthony Hoekema says:

> Note that God promises to give the land of Canaan not just to Abraham's descendants but also Abraham himself. Yet Abraham never owned as much as a square foot of ground in the land of Canaan (cf. Acts 7:5)—except for the burial cave which he had to purchase from the Hittites (see Gen.23). What, now, was Abraham's attitude with respect to this promise of the inheritance of the land of Canaan, which was never fulfilled in his lifetime? We get the answer to this question from the book of Hebrews. In chapter 11, verses 9–10, we read, "By faith he [Abraham] sojourned in the land of promise, as in a foreign land, living in tents with Isaac and Jacob, heirs with him of the same promise. For he looked forward to a city which has foundations, whose builder and maker is God." By "the city which has foundations" we are to understand the holy city or the new Jerusalem which will be found on the new earth. Abraham, in other words, looked forward to the new earth as the real fulfillment of

the inheritance which had been promised him—and so did the other patriarchs.[11]

All who believed the promise, like Abraham, knew that in this fallen world they were "strangers and exiles" (Heb 11:13). They belonged to the new covenant, their mediator was Christ, and their destiny was "the city of the living God, the heavenly Jerusalem" (Heb 12:22), a city in a land that was guaranteed because of another's obedience. In the words of Micah and Samuel Rehihan:

> We can state confidently that although all the Abrahamic promises typologically reveal the New Covenant, in their substance and essence they are distinct from it. Abraham knew that Canaan was not heaven."[12] In the Old Testament dispensation though the promise of salvation then, as now, had its foundations in Christ, yet to encourage the Old Testament saints to hope in the Celestial inheritance, God condescended to their weaknesses by exhibiting the promise of eternal life for their partial contemplation and enjoyment under the figure of temporal and terrestrial blessings. This temporal and terrestrial aspect of the covenant blessing has now passed away; it has dropped from the great house of salvation like scaffolding from a finished edifice.[13]

---

11. Hoekema, *The Bible and the Future*, 278.

12. Renihan, Micah and Samuel, "Reformed Baptist Covenant Theology and Biblical Theology", 480.

13. Jowett, *Encyclopaedia of Christianity*. Vol.7, 524. Taken from David Kingdon's *Children of Abraham*, 40

8

Abraham's Double Capacity

PRESBYTERIANS TELL US THAT the Abrahamic covenant, the covenant of circumcision, is, like the later Mosaic covenant, an administration of the covenant of grace, with, of course, the new covenant being the final administration of this one covenant of grace. Because children were members of the Abrahamic covenant through circumcision, so, they believe, the children of believers are members of the new covenant, only now baptism has replaced circumcision. If, however, the Abrahamic covenant was something other than an administration of the covenant of grace this entire line of reasoning becomes untenable.

Nehemiah Coxe writes:

> Abraham is to be considered in a double capacity: he is the father of all true believers and the father and root of the Israelite nation. God entered into a covenant with him for both these seeds and since they are formally distinguished from one another, their covenant interest must necessarily be different and fall under distinct consideration. The blessings appropriate to either must be conveyed in a way agreeable to their particular and respective covenant interest. And these things may not

be confounded without manifest hazard to the most important articles in the Christian religion.[1]

The Apostle states:

> Now the promises were made to Abraham and his offspring. It does not say, "And to offsprings," referring to many, but referring to one, "And to your offspring," who is Christ. (Gal 3:16)

Jesus Christ is the true seed of Abraham. Abraham's spiritual seed (plural) are saved because, like Abraham himself, they have believed in Abraham's promised *Seed* (singular) who is Jesus Christ (Gal 3:16).[2] These put their faith in him, and became God's spiritual sons through adoption, "For in Christ Jesus you are all sons of God through faith" (Gal 3:26). All of these were baptized, immersed or ingrafted into the body of Christ by the work of the Holy Spirit (v.27), and even though they physically found themselves under the old covenant, they were, nevertheless, also in receipt of the blessings which flow from the new covenant.

Entry into both the Abrahamic/old covenant was by natural birth, whereas entry into the new covenant is only through a new supernatural birth. It is not parental lineage and ethnicity or anything else of a physical nature which matters for entrance into the new covenant. To quote Sam Storms, "Having Abraham's blood in one's veins is not the primary consideration, but rather having Abraham's faith in one's heart."[3] Those in the nation of Israel who knew only a natural birth never became a "new creation" (Gal 6:15) and a "spiritual house . . . a holy priesthood to offer spiritual sacrifices acceptable to God through Jesus Christ" (1 Pet 2:5). They were never God's true people. To put this another way, there was essentially an Israel within Israel, or a spiritual Israel within physical Israel. As the Apostle says, "For not all who are descended from Israel belong to Israel" (Rom 9:6), or as John Owen puts it:

---

1. Coxe, *A Discourse of the Covenants*, 72–73.

2. Again I am following the KJV, referring to "seed," rather than the ESV which translates it as "offspring".

3. Storms, *Kingdom Come*, 208.

Abraham's Double Capacity

Answerably unto this twofold end of the separation of Abraham, there was a double seed allotted unto him;— *a seed according to the flesh*, separated unto the bringing forth of the Messiah according unto the flesh; and *a seed according to the promise*, that is, such as by faith should have interest in the promise, or all the elect of God. Not that these two seeds were always *subjectively* diverse, so that the seed separated to the bringing forth of the Messiah in the flash should neither in whole nor in part be also the seed according to the promise; or, on the contrary, that the seed according to the promise should none of it be his seed after the flesh. Our apostle declares the contrary in the instances of Isaac and Jacob, with the "remnant" of Israel that shall be saved, Rom. ix, x., xi. But sometimes the same seed of Abraham both according to the flesh and according to the promise; and the seed itself was diverse, those according to the flesh being not of the promise, and so on the contrary. Thus, Isaac and Jacob were the seed of Abraham according to the flesh, separated unto the bringing forth of the Messiah after the flesh, because they were his carnal posterity; and they were also of the seed of the promise, because by their own personal faith, they were interested in the covenant of Abraham their father.[4]

Charles Hodge grasped this essential fact, although he was and remained a paedobaptist. He clearly distinguished between the Patriarch's carnal and spiritual descendants:

> It is to be remembered that there were two covenants made with Abraham. By the one his natural descendants through Isaac, were constituted a commonwealth, an external community; by the other his spiritual descendants were constituted a church, [invisible of course, since, at that time, the only formal organization was that of the law.] The parties to the former covenant, were God, and the nation: to the other, God, and his true people. The promises of the national covenant were national blessings: the promises of the spiritual covenant (*i.e.*, the covenant of grace) were spiritual blessings, as reconciliation,

---

4. Owen, *Works*, 17, 121–22.

holiness and eternal life. The conditions of the one covenant [the old] were circumcision, and obedience to the law; the conditions of the other were, and ever have been, faith in the Messiah, as the seed of the woman, the Son of God, the Savior of the world. There cannot be a greater mistake than to confound the national covenant with the covenant of grace, [that is, the old covenant with the new] and the commonwealth found on the one, with the church founded on the other. When Christ came, the commonwealth was abolished, and there was nothing to put in its place. The church [now made visible] remained. There was no external covenant, nor promise of external blessings, on condition of external rites, and subjection. There was a spiritual society, with spiritual promises, on condition of faith in Christ. The church is, therefore, in its essential nature, a company of believers, and not an external society, requiring merely external profession as the condition of membership in the Church prescribed than that contained in the answer of Philip to the Eunuch who desired Baptist: "If thou believest with all thine heart, thou mayest. And he answered and said, I believe that Jesus is the Son of God." (Acts viii:37).[5]

The seeds or children of Abraham can then be placed into two categories. There are those who, like Abraham, believe in the promise. These constitute the spiritual seed, the "spiritual society," the true Israel of God. Then there are his natural carnal seed, and as we know, many, if not the majority of these refused to believe the promises of God and knew only the conditional covenant; one that spoke of only temporal blessings. They would never become participators in what lay beyond the shadows and types. While Abraham was the natural father of all his seeds he is, spiritually speaking, only the father of those who exercise faith in the promise, "Know then that it is those of faith who are the sons of Abraham" (Gal 3:7), "And if you are Christ's, then you are Abraham's offspring, heirs according to the promise" (v.29). The essential differences between Abraham's offspring who believed the promises of God and those who refused to do so is well expressed by Johnson:

    5. Hodge, Charles, *Princeton Review*, October, 1853

Abraham's Double Capacity

The physical seed are the *natural* children of Abraham; the spiritual seed are the *supernatural* children of Abraham. The physical seed were circumcised in the *flesh*; the spiritual seed have been circumcised in *heart*. The physical seed inherited an earthly land; the spiritual seed are heirs to a *heavenly* city whose builder and maker is God. The physical seed became a geopolitical nation, an earthly kingdom; the spiritual seed have been birthed into the *kingdom of God*.[6]

It was only Abraham's "supernatural" spiritual children who constituted the true church of God. This church has remained, and will continue to remain one, consisting only of those who place their faith in Abraham's *Seed* (Gal 3:16).

Nowhere is what Nehemiah Coxe called Abraham's double capacity[7] made clearer than in the ninth chapter of Romans.[8] Paul, after showing how God's purposes cannot be thwarted and that nothing can separate his people from the love of Christ, (Rom 8:37–39), envisaged the Jews questioning this fact because, as we know, not all Israel has been saved. The Jews were his "kinsman according to the flesh" (Rom 9:3), and Paul yearns to see them saved (v.2–3). However, in spite of their unsaved condition, he knows that the word of God has not failed (v.6) because not all those who are Israelites belong to the Israel of God. Yes, they might be Abraham's offspring according to the flesh, but, "it is not the children of the flesh who are the children of God, but the children of the promise are counted as offspring" (Rom 9:8). God was perfectly within his right to reject the Jews because the majority never constituted his true chosen people. As Charles Hodge puts it:

> [I]t was a common opinion among the Jews, that the promises of God being made to Abraham and his seed, all his natural descendants sealed as such by the rite of circumcision, would certainly inherit the blessings of the

---

6. Johnson, *Kingdom of God*, 58.
7. Coxe, *A Discourse of the Covenants*, 72.
8. Romans chapters 9–11 is Paul's theodicy—a vindication of God's dealings when there is so much evil in the world. In these chapters Paul is vindicating God when it seemed certain Jews that God's plan to save Israel had failed.

> Messiah's reign ... The reason why the rejection of the Jews involved no failure on the part of the divine promise, is, that the promise was not addressed to the mere natural descendants of Abraham. His object is to show that the promises made to the children of Abraham were not made to his natural descendants as such.[9]

Paul then goes to demonstrate that it is all according to the will of God and his sovereign choice as to who he will show mercy (v.15). God's rejection of carnal Israel and his plan for the Gentile world was what he had planned beforehand and revealed to the prophets of old (Rom 9:24–29). Again, Hodge explains this in a manner that fully accords with the Baptist theology:

> That God was at liberty to reject the Jews and to call the Gentiles, Paul argues, 1. By showing that the promises which he had made, and by which he had graciously bound himself, were not made to the natural descendants of Abraham as such, but to his spiritual seed. This is plain from the case Ishmael and Isaac; both were the children of Abraham, yet one was taken and the other left. And also from the case of Esau and Jacob. Though children of the same parents, and born at one birth, yet "Jacob have I loved and Esau have I hated." Is the language of God respecting them, verses 6–13[10]

John G. Reisinger makes an interesting comment concerning Hodge's position, one which shows the faulty hermeneutic employed by paedobaptists:

> How can Hodge not see that his paedobaptism makes the very same mistake the Jews made? If one really understands the ground upon which infant baptism rests, and read the above comments substituting 'Christian parents' for 'Jews,' it should be enlightening! Hodge wants to eliminate the Jews, as the natural seed, from the covenant made with Abraham because, as he says, "The promises were *not* made to the natural descendants of Abraham, but to his spiritual seed." However, Hodge then wants

9. Hodge, Charles, *A Commentary on Romans*, 303.
10. Hodge, *A Commentary on Romans*, 304–6

Abraham's Double Capacity

the identical covenant of Abraham to include the *natural descendants* of believers today. As a wise man once said, "Consistency is a gem of rare value."[11]

Presbyterians usually equate the church in the Old Testament with the nation, with Abraham's physical offspring. This, however, was never God's church. The true church existed within Israel but cannot be equated with Israel; it consisted only of those within Israel who believed. Only such as these constituted the true Jews, as the Apostle puts it, "For no one is a Jew who is merely one outwardly, nor is circumcision outward and physical. But a Jew is one inwardly, and circumcision is a matter of the heart, by the Spirit, not the letter" (Rom 2:28–29).

The Old Testament church was not replaced at Christ's coming.[12] The same church continues to grow as God's people from the Gentile world believe upon the lord Jesus Christ. The Gentiles are "no longer strangers and aliens, but . . . fellow citizens with the saints and members of the household of God," both having "access in one Spirit to the Father (Eph 2:18, 19). About the one faith, one church, John Owen states:

> Abraham, on the account of his faith, and not of his separation according to the flesh, was the father of all that believe, and heir of the world. And in the covenant made with him, as to that which concerns, not the bringing forth of the promised Seed according to the flesh, but as unto faith therein, and in the work of redemption to be performed thereby, lies the foundation of the church in all ages. Wheresoever this covenant is, and with whomsoever it is established, with them is the church; unto whom all the promises and privileges of the church do belong. Hence it was, that at the coming of the Messiah there was not one church taken away, and another set up in the room thereof; but the church continued the same, in

---

11. Reisinger, *Abrahams Four Seeds*, 98.

12. So-called replacement theology, or supersessionism, believes that the Old Testament church was replaced after Christ's redemptive work, with the Gentile church superseding the Jewish church. Such teaching is foreign to Reformed Baptists.

those what were the children of Abraham according to the faith. The Christian church is not another church, but the very same that was before the coming of Christ, having the same faith with it, and interested in the same covenant.[13]

With the arrival of Christ the old commonwealth of Israel was abolished; it had served its purpose. No longer was the physical seeds of Abraham (Israel) accorded any special status. The church, the assembly of those who profess faith in the *Seed* had come of age.

In his letter to the Galatians, the Apostle employs an allegory to highlight certain truths about Abraham's two seeds, the physical and natural. As we have seen, certain Jews were of the opinion that to be truly Christian it was necessary for believers to submit to circumcision. Paul saw the folly of this; these Jews were simply declaring their ignorance of the law. They were effectively putting the people back under the rigours of the old covenant and the slavery that this entailed when they had already entered into the freedom of the new covenant. The allegory (Gal 4:21–31) further demonstrates that the law or old covenant can lead only to bondage, and that true freedom comes only through the new covenant.

> Tell me, you who desire to be under the law, do you not listen to the law? For it is written that Abraham had two sons, one by a slave woman and one by a free woman. But the son of the slave was born according to the flesh, while the son of the free woman was born through promise. Now this may be interpreted allegorically: these women are two covenants. One is from Mount Sinai, bearing children for slavery; she is Hagar. Now Hagar is Mount Sinai in Arabia; she corresponds to the present Jerusalem, for she is in slavery with her children. But the Jerusalem above is free, and she is our mother. For it is written,
> "Rejoice, O barren one who does not bear;
> break forth and cry aloud, you who are not in labor!
> For the children of the desolate one will be more
> than those of the one who has a husband."
> Now you, brothers, like Isaac, are children of promise. But just as at that time he who was born according

---

13. Owen, *Hebrews*, 17, 123.

Abraham's Double Capacity

> to the flesh persecuted him who was born according to the Spirit, so also it is now. But what does the Scripture say? "Cast out the slave woman and her son, for the son of the slave woman shall not inherit with the son of the free woman."

The old covenant is represented by Ishmael and his mother, Hagar. Ishmael's mother was a "slave women" and he was born, not as the result of promise, but in the natural way, "born according to the flesh." Paul links Hagar to the old covenant which, as we shall see, was established at Mount Sinai. Those under this covenant are not free, but are born into slavery. This was because the old covenant was made with a sinful people and it promised earthly blessings based upon conditions the people were incapable of keeping. One such earthly blessing was the city of Jerusalem. However, far from achieving freedom under the law, "Jerusalem is in slavery with her children." The people were under a yoke that they were unable to bear (Acts 15:10). This is why elsewhere the Apostle speaks of the covenant being "the ministry of death" and a "ministry of condemnation" (2 Cor 3:7,9). This was the very thing those who were advocating circumcision failed to grasp. They were putting themselves under such a ministry when they had been made members of the "ministry of righteousness" (2 Cor 3:9). It simply made no sense.

Sarah, and her son Isaac correspond to the new covenant. Her children are born of promise, born free, and born into the Jerusalem of which the earthly city was put a type. Being Abraham's spiritual seed, they belong to what the writer to the Hebrews calls "the city of the living God, the heavenly Jerusalem" (Heb 11:22). About the contrast Jeffrey Johnson states:

> Paul contrasts the "Jerusalem, which is above," from the "Jerusalem which now is." This contrast shows the fundamental difference between Abraham's natural and spiritual seed. The "Jerusalem which is now" refers to the carnal descendants of Abraham, who are born after the flesh (a natural birth). The "Jerusalem which is

above," refers to the spiritual children of Abraham, who are born from above.[14]

This is the same point that Paul was making in Romans 9:6–9). Those born of promise, those who exercise faith, constitute the true Israel. Those who believe not, are those which constitute, and remain Abraham's natural offspring. Hence Paul's can say that

> not all who are descended from Israel belong to Israel,
> and not all are the children of Abraham
> because they are his offspring, but
> "Through Isaac shall your offspring be
> named." This means that it is not the children
> of the flesh who are the children
> of God, but "the children of the promise
> who are counted as offspring" (Rom. 9:6–8).

The Jews considered themselves to be the true children of Abraham simply because of their birth and their membership of the old covenant. They boasted that Abraham was their father, "We are the offspring of Abraham and have never been enslaved to anyone. How is it that you say, 'You will become free?'" (John 8:33). They failed to understand that one of the old covenant's functions was to teach them the essential fact that they were enslaved and in need of salvation from above (Rom 3:19–22). Jesus responded to the so-called teachers of the law, saying, ". . . truly, truly, I say to you, 'everyone who practices sin is a slave to sin. The slave does not remain in the house forever; the son remains forever. So if the Son sets you free, you will be free indeed'" (John 8:34–36). The Jews were mistaking the type—the old covenant, for the antitype—the new covenant. The law, with its conditional this-worldy blessings and cursings, was but a type and shadow of the blessings which are guaranteed for all those who believed in the promise. It is only those who are born from above and placed into Christ who are sons, only these will remain in the house forever. Those who remain in the flesh will be like Hagar and her sons who received no inheritance but were cast out. About this essential truth Nehemiah Coxe states:

---

14. Johnson, *The Fatal Flaw*, 87.

Abraham's Double Capacity

Hagar was a type of Mount Sinai and the legal covenant established there. Ishmael was a type of the carnal seed of Abraham under that covenant. Sarah was a type of the new Jerusalem, the gospel church founded on the covenant of grace. Isaac was a type of the true members of that church who are born of the Spirit, being converted by the power of the Holy Spirit for the fulfilling of the promise of the Father to Jesus Christ the mediator. And the ejection of Hagar and Ishmael was to prefigure the abrogation of the Sinaitic Covenant and the dissolving of the Jewish church-state so that the inheritance of spiritual blessings might be clearly passed down to the children of God by faith in Jesus Christ.[15]

Like all analogies, it can be caricatured, for example, Chris Villi, in criticizing the Reformed Baptist understanding of the passage states: "One seemingly obvious weakness in their arguments from this passage for two non-mixed, distinct seeds is that Ishmael was never a member of the covenant inwardly or outwardly whereas Isaac was both."[16] He is, however, literalizing the allegory. If we do this much of what Paul is saying here fails to make sense, for example, what does Hagar have to do with Mount Sinai? Paul is using an allegory, not because it directly corresponds to history, but to teach an important truth about the old and new covenants.

Let me leave this chapter with a quote from St Augustine, a man who grasped precisely what the text means:

> This interpretation of the passage, handed down to us with apostolic authority, shows how we ought to understand the Scriptures of the two covenants—the old and the new. One portion of the earthly city became an image of the heavenly city, not having a significance of its own, but signifying another city, and therefore serving, or "being in bondage." For it was founded not for its own sake, but to prefigure another city; and this shadow of a city was also itself foreshadowed by another preceding

---

15. Coxe, *A Discourse of the Covenants*, 130–31.

16. Villi, https://www.jesuspaidinfull.com/Documents/CVilli_1689_Federalism_Paper.pdf

figure. For Sarah's handmaid Agar, and her son, were an image of this image. And as the shadows were to pass away when the full light came, Sarah, the free woman, who prefigured the free city (which again was also prefigured in another way by that shadow of a city Jerusalem), therefore said, "Cast out the bond woman and her son; for the son of the bond woman shall not be heir with my son Isaac," or, as the apostle says, "with the son of the free woman." In the earthly city, then, we find two things—its own obvious presence, and its symbolic presentation of the heavenly city. And this was typified in the two sons of Abraham,—Ishmael, the son of Agar the handmaid, being born according to the flesh, while Isaac was born of the free woman Sarah, according to the promise. Both, indeed, were of Abraham's seed; but the one was begotten by natural law, the other was given by gracious promise. In the one birth, human action is revealed; in the other, a divine kindness comes to light.[17]

---

17. Augustine, *City of God*, Book 15.

9

The Sinaitic Covenant

ONE CANNOT BUT AGREE with the words of Jonathan Edwards, "there is perhaps no part of divinity attended with so much intricacy, and wherein orthodox divines do so much differ as stating the precise agreement and difference between the two dispensations of Moses and Christ."[1] Throughout history, there has been no shortage of theories as to the covenant's meaning. According to Anthony Burgess:

> In expressing this covenant there is a difference among the Learned: some make the law a covenant of works, and upon that ground it is abrogated: others call it a subservient covenant to the covenant of grace, and make it occasionally, as it were, introduced, to put more luster and splendour upon grace: Others call it a mixt covenant of works and grace: but it is hardly to be understood as possible, much less as true. I therefore think that opinion true . . . that the law given by Moses was a covenant of grace.[2]

Many, if not most, Presbyterians, in keeping with the teachings of the Westminster Confession, believe the Mosaic covenant to be an

---

1. Edwards, *Works*, 160.
2. Burgess, *Vindiciae Legis*, 39.

Reformed Baptist Covenant Theology

administration of the one covenant of grace,[3] of the same substance as the new covenant. As R. Scott Clark puts it, "The New Covenant is not heaven but the last provisional administration of the covenant of grace before glory."[4] In contrast, all Reformed Baptists who adhere to the 1689 Confession believe the Mosaic covenant to be of works.

As I said earlier, John Owen puts forward a view of the old covenant which thoroughly accords with what Baptists teach. After examining the Presbyterian understanding he concluded that what is taught in Scripture:

> can hardly be accommodated unto a *twofold administration* of the same covenant. we must grant *two distinct covenants* rather than a twofold administration of the same covenant merely, to be intended. We must, I say, do so, provided always that the way of reconciliation and salvation was the same under both. But it will be said,- and with great presence of reason, for it is that which is the sole foundation they all build upon, who then allow a twofold administration of the same covenant.,- 'That this being the principal end of a divine covenant, it the way of reconciliation and salvation be the same under both, then indeed are they for the substance of them but one.' And I grant that this would inevitably follow, if it were so equally by virtue of them both. If reconciliation and salvation by Christ were to be obtained not only under the old covenant, but by virtue thereof, then it must be the same for substance with the new. But this is not so; for no reconciliation with God, nor salvation could be obtained by virtue of the old covenant, or the administration of it, as our apostle disputes at large, though all believers were reconciled, justified, and saved, by virtue of the promise, whilst they were under the covenant.[5]

---

3. A number of Presbyterians, whilst believing the Abrahamic covenant to be of grace, believe the Mosaic covenant to be of works, e.g., Michael Horton. See also, *The Law is not of Faith*

4. Clark, Did the Covenant of Grace Begin in the New Covenant? www.Heidelblog.net

5. Owen, *Works*, 22, 76–77.

The Sinaitic Covenant

Presbyterians are faced with something of a problem when the Apostle places the old and new covenants in opposition, e.g., 2 Cor 3:3–7; Rom 6:14; Gal 2:21; 3:18 etc. To get around this they suggest that in these passages the Apostle is referring to the original covenant of works. This, however, is simply not the case. These texts are speaking, not of the covenant as made with Adam, but the Sinaitic or old covenant. Therefore, when reference is here made to the old covenant I shall have in mind not the Adamic covenant nor the Old Testament as a whole, but specifically the covenant made with Moses at Sinai. The very same covenant spoken of In Jeremiah 31, when the Lord took the people of Israel "by the hand to bring them out of the land of Egypt," the "covenant that they broke" (Jere 31:32).

The Mosaic covenant, like the covenant of circumcision, was a covenant of works. It "continued the natural aspects of the Abrahamic Covenant by expanding the condition to include obedience to the whole law."[6] According to Alan Connor:

> It is vitally connected to the Abrahamic Covenant. Moses taught that the covenant established with Israel when they came out of Egypt was but an extension and furthering of God's covenant with Abraham. God promised Abraham that he would become a great nation, be given the promised land, and be a blessing to all the nations. The Mosaic Covenant expands upon these elements and provides the covenant ethic by which Israel was to possess and enjoy the promised land (Deuteronomy 6:1; 8:6–7).[7]

Or, as Micah and Samuel Renihan put it:

> The Mosaic Covenant was added and attached to the Abrahamic Covenant in such a way that it further conditioned the enjoyment of the Abrahamic blessings. God immutably promised Abraham that the covenant blessings would be realized. The extent to which those

---

6. Johnson, *The Fatal Flaw*, 224.
7. Connor, *Covenant Children Today*, 42.

Reformed Baptist Covenant Theology

blessings would be enjoyed, however, depended upon the obedience of the people of Israel.[8]

The covenant of circumcision and the Mosaic or Sinaitic covenant go hand in hand, being essentially different sides of the same coin. As we saw earlier, the law was in operation before Sinai, but at Sinai, to quote Pink:

> God gave Israel a full declaration of His claims upon them and what He required of them, providing a "constitution" which had in view naught but their own good and the glorifying of His great name; the whole being ratified by a solemn covenant. This was a decided advance on all that had gone before, and marked another step forward in the unfolding of the divine plan.[9]

The Mosaic covenant was essentially the same in substance as the covenant established with Abraham, only at Sinai it was tweaked for the governance of a nation.

Believing both covenants to be of grace,[10] Peter Golding states what the majority of Presbyterians believe:

> Nowhere is the *new* covenant contrasted invidiously with the Abrahamic. Christ made the *Mosaic* covenant 'old', when he referred to the new covenant in his blood, but the Abrahamic covenant is never said to be abrogated, it still stands and comes to fruition in the *new*. Consequently, the New Testament does not say that the Abrahamic covenant passed away. Rather the opposite: the covenant with Abraham blesses all the nations of the earth, and Christian believers of every race are described as 'children of Abraham' (Gen. 12:3; Gal. 3:29).[11]

---

8. Renihan, Micah and Samuel, "Reformed Baptist Covenant Theology and Biblical Theology", 480.

9. Pink. *The Divine Covenants*, 104.

10. A number of Presbyterians believe the Mosaic covenant to be one of works, e.g., Michael Horton. Here they take a position similar to the reformed Baptists. They still, however, believe the Abrahamic covenant to be of grace, and they do not distinguish between Genesis 15 and 17.

11. Golding, *Covenant Theology*, 153.

The Sinaitic Covenant

As I said previously, it is vital to distinguish between the covenant promised to Abraham in Genesis 15, which was ratified in the promise, and the covenant established with him in Genesis 17. The hallmark of the latter was circumcision. Let us remind ourselves of exactly what the Scripture says about this:

> And God said to Abraham, "As for you, you shall keep my covenant, you and your offspring after you throughout the generations. This is my covenant, which you shall keep between me and you and your offspring after you. Every male among you shall be circumcised. You shall be circumcised in the flesh of your foreskins, and it shall be a sign of the covenant between me and you (Gen 17:9–11)

As Paul made clear in his letter to the Galatians, circumcision has been abrogated, and with it the covenant established with Abraham. Golding is taking the typical Presbyterian understanding which lumps what is said in Genesis 12, 15, and 17 together to represent one covenant of grace, and since a covenant once ratified cannot be annulled or added to (Gal 3:15), then the Mosaic covenant too must be of grace. They fail to distinguish between the promise revealed to Abraham and the covenant of works established with him.

When Paul alludes in Galatians 3:17 to a covenant that cannot be annulled it seems most unlikely that he is speaking of the covenant of circumcision in Genesis 17. I say this because his opponents in the Galatian church were demanding that all believers be circumcised. For the Apostle to then appeal to the covenant of circumcision would be to play into their hands. They would simply have said that the covenant was still in force and that the rite was still a necessity. Furthermore, we saw earlier, the rite implied more than something performed on the skin. It spoke of the law of God, and it was to this covenant that the Mosaic law was added and attached, and just as the Mosaic law was abrogated with the coming of Christ, so was the Abrahamic covenant of circumcision. In Galatians 3:17, the Apostle is simply saying that the law which came in 430 years after the promise cannot change or annul the thing promised, and, of course, the promise he is alluding to is that found in Genesis 15.

When speaking of the old covenant one might ask why Paul alludes to the Mosaic covenant and not the Abrahamic covenant. The answer lies in the fact that, as Micah and Samuel Renihan say, ". . . the Mosaic Covenant controls both the Abrahamic and the Davidic Covenants, it is the primary referent point of the New Testament when speaking about the Old Covenant."[12] The law in all its details was delivered through Moses and not Abraham. The specific judical laws governing Jewish life in Israel were not revealed prior to Sinai. The Apostle is addressing the Jewish tendency to believe in the efficacy of the Mosaic economy in regard to their salvation.

The Jews did not separate the law into the three categories, namely, the sacrificial, judicial, and moral, that was only done much later. They saw the law as a complete package. Contrary to what many say, the Jews were not guilty of believing that the way to God was by keeping the commandments perfectly, rather, they wrongly assumed that when they did sin their transgressions could be catered for through the various animal sacrifices, irrespective of their inner state. As we shall see, while the sacrifices, when offered correctly, could effect things temporal, they could not cleanse the conscience (Heb 9:9). However, even concerning things temporal, Israel usually only succeeded in bringing the wrath of God upon itself. When Paul reminds believers that no one can be justified by the works of the law (Rom 3:20; Gal 2:16, 3:11), he is alluding to the entire Mosaic system, i.e., trying to keep God's commandments and statutes, falling short, and relying on the various sacrifices to find forgiveness. This was to do the law. Their problem was that they divorced the law from the Christ to whom it pointed; they were relying on the types, and missing entirely the antitype. The Jews had effectively made the law an end in itself rather than a means to an end, an end of which is Christ. They failed to grasp that salvation

---

12. Renihan, Micah and Samuel, "Reformed Baptist Covenant Theology and Biblical Theology", 482.

The Sinaitic Covenant

lay in another covenant, one in which "Christ is the end of the law for righteousness to everyone who believes" (Rom 10:4).

In a critical review of Pascal Denault's book, Chris Villi, in regard to Particular Baptists, comments,

> To them, the old covenant was in no way an administration of the Covenant of Grace; instead, it was a different substance altogether. When pondering the contours of this position, one must wonder about the purpose of the Old Covenant. How could God's primary way of relating to His people prior to the New Covenant be devoid of grace?[13]

No Reformed Baptist would say that the old covenant was devoid of grace. While it was not itself an administration of the covenant of grace, it still, nevertheless, contained grace and pointed to salvific grace in the promise. The very fact that God gave Israel the land, that he brought the people back from exile, and that he spoke of the Christ through his prophets etc., is all of grace. As Paul expresses it, "they were entrusted with the oracles of God" (Rom 3:2), "to them belong the adoption, the glory, the covenants, the giving of the law, the worship, and the promises. To them belong the patriarchs, and from their race, according to the flesh, is the Christ, who is God over all, blessed forever. Amen" (Rom 9:4–5). The whole purpose of the old covenant was to lead sinners to the new covenant in Christ. In itself it was a "ministry of death, carved in letters on stone" (2 Cor 3:7), a ministry that brought only condemnation (v.9). In all this, the law was a diagnostic tool of grace which served to make sinners aware of their need for a remedy.

Some are of the opinion that we have denuded the law of all salvific grace because we say that it was a covenant of works that promised only temporal blessings upon obedience. Nothing could be further from the truth. It needs to be remembered that in those times, God was calling individuals from out of carnal Israel, regenerating, justifying, and uniting them to Christ, i.e., making them participants in the future new covenant. Israel was not simply to

---

13. Villi, https://www.jesuspaidinfull.com/Documents/CVilli_1689_Federalism_Paper.pdf

Reformed Baptist Covenant Theology

preserve the Messianic line, but constituted a people unto whom God revealed his promise in a unique way. One might think of the old covenant as an evangelistic sermon. The purpose of which is to inform sinners about God's righteous requirements, to make known his divine displeasure for all who fall short of his glory, and to reveal his own remedy for sin. The old covenant does all three things. The Israelites would never keep the conditions necessary to secure continuance in the earthly land, how much less could they be expected to, through their own obedience, enter into God's celestial land. They brought upon their heads only God's displeasure, and in the very midst of this God provided an elaborate sacrificial system which, although it could not take away sin, spoke of one who would be able to do so. God also raised up prophets who pointed to his remedy in the coming Redeemer. To then think that this covenant is divorced from grace is to completely misunderstand its function in the purposes of God.

Yes, God had redeemed the people from their bondage in Egypt. He had led them through the Red Sea and sustained them, all because of his free unmerited grace. In grace, he provided Israel a land to live in, but as mentioned earlier, remaining in the land was far from guaranteed; it would be conditional upon keeping God's commandments. As Meredith Kline points out, the Mosaic covenant "made inheritance to be by law, not by promise-not by faith, but by works."[14] At Sinai the Lord clearly laid out the conditional nature of his covenant:

> Now, therefore, if you will indeed obey my voice and keep my covenant, you shall be my treasured possession among all peoples, for all the earth is mine; **6** and you shall be to me a kingdom of priests and a holy nation.' These are the words that you shall speak to the people of Israel. (Exodus.19:5–6)

There's a tendency to read Exodus 19:5 while paying scant regard to the important little word "if". Israel never did become a "kingdom of priests and a holy nation" because it utterly failed

---

14. Kline, *By Oath Consigned*, 23. Eermans, 1968.

The Sinaitic Covenant

to obey God's voice and keep his covenant. The same can be seen with one of the great promises running through Scripture, namely, "I will be your God and you will be my People," Gen 17:7; Ex 6:7; Jere 7:23, 31, 30:22; Ezek 11:20 etc. This again was conditional. The Lord said to Jeremiah, "But this thing I commanded them, saying, Obey my voice, and I will be your God, and you shall be my people: and walk you in all the ways that I have commanded you, that it may be well unto you" (Jere 7:23). Again, in Ezekiel, we read, "That they may walk in my statutes, and keep my rules and obey them. And they shall be my people, and I will be their God" (Ezek 11:20). Israel's problem was simply that it was unable to obey the Lord, just as Joshua had foretold, saying "to the people, 'You are not able to serve the LORD, for he is a holy God; He is a jealous God; he will not forgive your transgressions or your sins'" (Josh 24:19). The promise found its fulfilment, however, is all those who believed. God was their God and they were his people because of Christ's future work, the benefits of which were retroactively applied to them.

Many Presbyterians argue that the law was given to an already saved people for their sanctification. They were, in other words, to keep the law not to merit blessings, but out of gratitude for what they had already been given. They look at, say, the Passover in Exodus 12, where the families daubed blood on their lintels and doorposts, blood that the Angel of the Lord saw and passed over, as proof that those who were spared the wrath were saved spiritually. This, however, is simply not the case. It is true that the people of Israel had been spared God's immediate wrath and had been redeemed from their bondage in Egypt, but it is false to maintain that this redemption was spiritual. It instead marked the temporal, typical redemption of a sinful people. Likewise, the manna which the Lord provided (Ex 16; Num 11) for the Israelites while in the desert pointed to spiritual food for those who had faith and saw behind the physical, but, no doubt, for the vast majority it only provided sustenance for their physical bodies. About the types and antitypes, Reisinger comments:

> The redemption from Egypt does not equal justification by faith. National 'adoption' does not equal 'sons of God.' Election as a nation among nations is not equal to "chosen in Christ before the foundation of the world" unto salvation. The national and physical redemption from Egypt by blood is not equal to the eternal spiritual redemption by the blood of Christ; and "called out of Egypt" is not the same as the effectual call in Romans 1:7. An *unsaved* Israelite was just as much 'redeemed' from Egypt as a believing Israelite. Every *unsaved* Israelite could say, "God loved me in a way he did not love the Egyptians, and he redeemed me from Egypt by his might power because I am the seed of Abraham." However, when a Christian uses the identical words, they mean something entirely different.[15]

The types were always subservient to the antitype; they must never be viewed as an end in themselves. The law itself was not given for the sanctification of the truly saved, but because of the sinfulness of the unsaved. Again, speaking of Israel in reference to certain affirmations made by Presbyterians, James Haldane says:

> Nothing can be more fallacious than the affirmation, that the church was the same in all ages. If by this is meant that God had a people in every age, who have been equally dear to him, and who have lived by faith, it is true. But those who make the assertion mean, that formally the nation of Israel was the church of God in a spiritual sense, which is manifestly contrary to fact. The great body of people were alienated from God in their minds and by wicked works; and among other nations he had some, perhaps many true worshippers. Nor was it the duty of the latter to join the church of Israel. They might or they might not. But if Israel was the church of God, as believers are now are, it would surely have been the duty of all God's children to have come and dwelt among them, which it was not; therefore the assertion that the church has been the same in all ages is entirely unfounded.[16]

---

15. Reisinger, *Abraham's Four Seeds*, 71.
16. Haldane A. James, *Galatians*, 437.

The Sinaitic Covenant

The people of Israel, while they received temporal blessings from God were still a people under the original covenant of works, and stood, like the rest of humanity, condemned by this covenant. For the majority, those who knew only the old covenant, the one promised, the *Seed* of Abraham, became a "stone of stumbling, a rock of offence" (1 Pet 2:8). However, all who believed, who were in receipt of new covenant blessings, became, as Peter says, a "chosen race, a royal priesthood, a holy nation, a people for his own possession, that you might proclaim the excellencies of him who called you out of darkness into his marvellous light" (1 Pet 2:9). It is only for those in Christ that the promises find their yes (2 Cor 1:20).

The Mosaic law held out no hope of eternal life on condition of obedience. In other words, it was not an exact republication of the original covenant of works? Jeffrey Johnson, a Reformed Baptist, believes that it does indeed promise eternal life. Taking his cue from Christ's encounter with the lawyer in Luke 10, he writes, "according to the terms of the Mosaic covenant, eternal life was dependent upon the establishment of perfect righteousness."[17] As we know, the lawyer approached Christ and asked how he might obtain eternal life (v.27). Jesus responded, saying, "love the Lord your God with all your heart and with all your soul and with all your strength and with all your mind, and your neighbour as yourself." Was Jesus here actually saying that it would be possible, should the lawyer keep the law, eternal life would be his? It is, however, questionable that this is what Jesus meant. Yes, the law reminded Israel of the original covenant's promise but it held out no possibility of it being realised. It could, as it were, dangle the unobtainable before the eyes of sinful man, but could do nothing whatsoever to help him achieve it. This was because sin had already entered in. The law was effectively weakened by the flesh (Rom 8:3). As Owen expresses it, "Nor had this covenant of Sinai any promise of eternal life annexed to it, as such, but only the promise inseparable from the covenant of works which it revived, saying, "Do this, and live."[18] By "revived" Owen appears to mean that the promise

---

17. Johnson, *The Kingdom of God*, 60.
18. Owen, *Hebrews*, Vol. 22, 78.

referred to in the Sinai covenant served to remind the people of the promise man had forfeited by his disobedience to the original covenant of works.

Interestingly, Jesus did not say that the man would attain eternal life but that he would live. Jesus was directing him, no doubt, to Leviticus 18:5 and the temporal blessing of a long earthly life, which, in the words of Meyer, is "equivalent to the Deuteronomic lengthening of days . . . to an abundant life in the promised land."[19] Jesus was essentially pointing out the impossibility of keeping the law. The lawyer could not keep the Mosaic law to attain temporal blessings then how much less could he keep it to attain blessings of an eternal nature. Furthermore, even if he had kept the law perfectly from the time of his encounter with Jesus, it would have availed him little. As we have seen, he already stood condemned because of Adam's sin and his own many sins. As Owen reminds us:

> It is true, that he who is once a sinner, if he should afterward yield all that perfect obedience unto God that the law requires, could not thereby obtain the benefit of the promise of the covenant. But the sole reason of it is, because he is *antecedently a sinner*, and so obnoxious unto the curse of the law; and no man can be obnoxious unto its curse and have a right unto its promise at the same time.[20]

The old covenant was certainly not given to Israel to provide an alternative way of salvation, and it in no way altered the promise given to our first parents, and later ratified to Abraham, a promise which was "established as containing the only way and means of salvation of sinners."[21] To quote Buchanan:

> The addition of the Law was not intended to alter either the ground, or the method, of the sinner's justification, by substituting obedience to the Law for faith in the Promise; for the Law which was originally 'ordained unto

---

19. Meyer, *The End of the Law*, 218.
20. Owen, *Works*, 5, 243.
21. Owen, *Works*, 5, 78.

The Sinaitic Covenant

> life' was now found, by reason of sin, 'to be unto death;' but it was now 'added,' and promulgated anew with awful sanctions amidst the thunderings of lightnings of Sinai, to impress the Jews, and through them the Church at large, with a sense of the holiness and justice of Him with whom they had to do,-of the spirituality and extent of that obedience which they owed to Him,-of the number and heinousness of their sins,-and of their utter inability to escape the wrath and curse of God, otherwise than by taking refuge in the free promise of His grace.[22]

Although the law was subservient to the promise, it was itself an entirely different covenant from that through which salvific grace is given. Being a separate covenant that came in alongside the promise, the old covenant contained its own promises and punishments, as spelt out in Deuteronomy 27–30. The blessings had to do with life in earthly Canaan, safety from her enemies, healthy crops and longevity etc. Whereas the punishments concerned famines, disease, sickness and, eventually exile. Both blessings and punishments were of an entirely temporal nature. In this regard, the law was

> considered as a national covenant, by which their continued possession of the land of Canaan, and of all their privileges under the Theocracy, was left to depend on their external obedience to it,-might be called a national Covenant of Works, since their temporal welfare was suspended on the condition of their continued adherence to it; but in that aspect of it, it had no relation to the spiritual salvation of individuals, otherwise that as this might be affected by their retaining, or forfeiting, their outward privileges and means of grace[23]

Those Israelites, however, who embraced the promise in faith, like Abraham, Isaac and Jacob etc., belonged to the new covenant, which, as we saw earlier, was promised to Abraham before any conditional covenant was made with him. All who believed looked not to the earthly blessings that were dependent on an obedience

---

22. Buchanan, *The Doctrine of Justification*, 38.
23. Buchanan, *The Doctrine of Justification*, 38.

Reformed Baptist Covenant Theology

the nation would never provide, but to blessings that were assured because of Christ's obedience. They looked "to a city that has foundations, whose designer and builder is God" (Heb 11:10).

About the old covenant, Owen say:

> This covenant thus made, with these ends and promises did never save or condemn any man eternally. All that lived under the administration of it did attain eternal life, or perished forever, *not by virtue of this covenant*, as formally such. It did, indeed, revive the commanding power and sanction of the first covenant of works ... it directed also unto the promise which was the instrument of life and salvation unto all that did believe. But as unto what it had of its own, it was confined unto things temporal.[24]

According to St Augustine:

> That testament, however, which is properly called the Old, and was given on Mount Sinai, only earthly happiness is expressly promised. Accordingly ... into which the nation, after being led through the wilderness, was conducted, is called the land of promise, wherein peace and royal power, and gaining of victories over enemies, and an abundance of children and of fruits of the ground, and gifts of a similar kind are the promises of the Old Testament. And these, indeed, are figures of the spiritual blessings which appertain to the New Testament; but yet the man who lives under God's law with those earthly blessings for his sanction, is precisely the heir of the Old Testament, for just such rewards are promised and given to him, according to the terms of the Old Testament, as are the objects of his desire according to the condition of the old man.[25]

One should remember that when Augustine says "Old Testament" it is the old covenant he has in mind. Martin Luther, the father of the Reformation, agreeing with Augustine, states:

---

24. Buchanan, *The Doctrine of Justification*, 85.
25. Augustine, *Proceedings on Pelagius*, 13 (v).

The Sinaitic Covenant

the old testament given through Moses was not a promise of forgiveness of sins or eternal things, but of temporal things, namely, of the land of Canaan, by which no man was renewed in spirit to lay hold of the heavenly inheritance. Wherefore also it was necessary that, a figure of Christ, a dumb beast should be slain, in whose blood the same testament might be confirmed as the blood corresponded to the testament and the sacrifice corresponded to the promise. But here Christ says "the new testament in my blood" (Luke 22:20; 1 Cor. 11:25), not somebody else's but his own, by which grace is promised through the Spirit for the forgiveness of sins, that we may obtain the inheritance.[26]

The Mosaic law, whilst being a covenant of works, did not abrogate or replace the original covenant of works. The old covenant did, however, underscore the need for blood to be shed because of sin. The many sacrifices were powerless to take away sin and guilt. The writer to the Hebrews says that the "gifts and sacrifices are offered that cannot perfect the conscience of the worshiper, but deal only with food and drink and various washings, regulations for the body imposed until the time of reformation." (Heb 9:9–10). They were themselves patterned after the prototype, serving as "a copy and shadow of the heavenly things" (Heb 8:5), i.e., the new covenant.

Some Baptists are of the opinion that God required less obedience from the nation of Israel than he required from the individual Israelite. In regard to the eternal salvation of the individual Israelite the Lord required a perfect obedience, an obedience he was incapable of rendering. Without this there could be no spiritual blessings. Yet in regard to national Israel's position under the old covenant, God would accept a less than perfect obedience:

> The Sinaitic covenant in no way interfered with the divine administration of either the everlasting covenant of grace (toward the elect) nor the Adamic covenant of works (which all by nature lie under); it being quite another religion. Whether the individual Israelites were heirs of blessing under the former, or under the curse of

26. Luther, *The Babylonian Captivity of the Church*.

Reformed Baptist Covenant Theology

the latter, in no wise hindered or affected Israel's being as a people under this national regime, which respected not inward and eternal blessings, but only outward and temporal interests. Nor did God in entering into this arrangement with Israel mock their impotency or tantalize them with vein hopes, any more than He does so now, when it still holds good that "righteousness exalteth a nation; but sin is a reproach to nations (Prov 14:34). Though it be true that Israel miserably failed to keep to their national engagements and brought down upon themselves the penalties which God had threatened, nevertheless, the obedience which He required of them was not obviously and hopelessly impracticable: nay, there were bright periods in their history when it was fairly rendered, and the fruits of it were manifestly enjoyed by them.[27]

Such an understanding invokes the objection: "that God, who is infinitely holy and whose prerogative it is to search the heart, could ever be satisfied with an outward and general obedience, which in the case of many would be hollow and insincere"[28]? Pink answers this by suggesting that nations are in a special category and God demands a lower level of obedience:

> Very simply: this would be true of individuals as such, but not necessarily so where nations are concerned. And why not?, it may be asked? For this reason: because nations as such have only a temporary existence; therefore they must be rewarded or punished in this present world, or not at all! This being so, the kind of obedience required from them is lower than from individuals, whose rewards and punishments shall be eternal.[29]

God had blessed Israel more than any other nation, yet in spite of this it had miserably failed, and, as Pink reminds us, "The lesson supplied thereby for all succeeding generations of the human race is written in unmistakable language: If Israel failed under the national covenant or outward and general obedience, how

---

27. Pink, *The Divine Covenants*, 108.
28. Pink *The Divine Covenants*, 109.
29. Pink *The Divine Covenants*, 109.

The Sinaitic Covenant

impossible it is for any member of Adam's depraved offspring to render spiritual and perfect obedience."[30]

Others, and here I will allude to the Congregationalist, John Owen because his view reflects that of many Reformed Baptists, disagree with the notion that a perfect God could ever accept anything less than a perfect obedience:

> I cannot but somewhat admire how it came into the heart or mind of any man to think or say, that God ever gave a law or laws, precept or precepts, that should "respect the outward man only, and the regulation of external duties." A thought of it is contrary to all the essential properties of the nature of God, and meet only the ingenerate apprehensions of him unsuited unto all his glorious excellencies. The life and foundation of all the laws under the Old Testament was, "Thou shalt love the LORD thy God with all thy soul;" without which no outward obedience was ever accepted with him.[31]

I would suggest that instead of two levels of obedience, one should consider two levels as pertaining to the sacrifices offered. A type must possess some degree of efficacy if it is to truly typify that which is perfectly efficacious unto the ends for which it is provided. In other words, the various sacrifices, when offered correctly, must have secured something for Israel because they were copies, albeit, imperfect, of Christ's perfect sacrifice.

> But there are two things to be considered in those sins which God had appointed that atonement should be made for. The first was, *the external, temporal punishment which was due unto them,* according to the place which the law or covenant had in the polity or commonwealth of Israel. The other, that *eternal* punishment which was due unto every sin by the law, as the rule of all moral obedience; "for the wages of sin is death." In the first of these the *person of the sinner,* in all his outward circumstances, his life, his goods, his liberty, and the like was concerned. In the latter, his conscience, or inward

---

30. Pink, *The Divine Covenants*, 111.
31. Owen, *Works*, 22, 87.

> man alone was so. And as unto the first of them, the gifts and sacrifices mentioned, being rightly offered, were able in themselves, "ex opera operato," to free the sinner from all temporal, political inconvenience or detriment, so as that his life and inheritance should be continued in the land of Canaan, or his state preserved entire in the commonwealth of Israel. This the apostle here tacitly acknowledgeth, namely, that the gifts and sacrifices were able to free the sinner from temporal punishment, and give him outward peace and possessions. But as unto the latter, wherein *conscience* was concerned, he denies they had any such efficacy.[32]

Those who offered the sacrifices sincerely, short of having faith in what they typified, could secure temporal blessings. They would, however, still be spiritually unsaved and under God's wrath. It was only those who saw Christ's day, who put their faith in the *Seed* of Abraham, who knew salvation and peace with God, not because of the many gifts and sacrifices, but because of their faith in Christ's future sacrifice. In the copies they saw the prototype. This is a very difficult subject, and whilst I would go along with the second of the above views, it may, in fact, be something of both, e.g., two levels of obedience and sacrifice.

All in Israel were by birth or otherwise members of the old covenant. This included both those who knew only fleshly circumcision, i.e., those whose hearts remained uncircumcised, and spiritual Israel, that Israel within Israel, which consisted of those whose hearts were circumcised by the Spirit of God. The latter would have been beneficiaries of the future new covenant through faith, while also being members of the old covenant. Whilst their salvation was assured because of their membership of the covenant that Christ kept and of which he is mediator, they could, nevertheless, still find themselves subject to the law's temporal punishments. For example, if they committed a crime, say like that committed by Moses when he killed the Egyptian (Ex 2:11–22), they could be put to death. The law of an "eye for eye, tooth for tooth, hand for hand, foot for foot" (Ex 21:24) applied as much to the saved Israelite as

32. Owen, *Works*, 22, 249.

The Sinaitic Covenant

to the unsaved. This would not, however, alter the fact that he is in Christ and secure in his salvation. Furthermore, when the nation suffered because of its sin, so too did those in the nation who believed. They were not immune to the law's temporal structures:

> Were not Moses and Aaron, for their disobedience, hindered from entering into the land of Canaan, as well as others? Num. XX:12. And was not Josiah, for his disobedience to God's command, slain in the valley of Megiddo? 2 Chron. XXXV, 21, 22. Therefore assure yourself, that when believers in the Old Testament did transgress God's commandments, God's temporal wrath went out against them, and was manifest in temporal calamities that befell them as well as others, Numb.Xvi, 46. Only there was a difference, the believers' temporal blessings had no eternal blessings included in them, and their temporal calamities had no eternal calamities included in them, following them.[33]

So while they believers were under the Mosaic law's temporary strictures, they were, nevertheless secure in regard to their eternal destiny. They knew that

> No reconciliation with God, nor salvation could be obtained by virtue of the old covenant, or the administration of it, as our apostle disputes at large, though *all believers were reconciled, justified and saved, by virtue of the promise, whilst they were under the old covenant*.[34]

While the old covenant spoke of only temporal things, it did, nevertheless, encourage sinners to look beyond itself; being subservient to and a facilitator of the promise:

> . . . every single element of the Mosaic economy typologically revealed and set before the eyes of the Jews the covenant of grace wherein true righteousness, true forgiveness of sins, and true holiness could be found, Since tenure in the land was what was in view in the Mosaic law, offences against that covenant could be addressed

---

33. Fisher, *Marrow of Modern Divinity*, 78.
34. Owen, *Works* 22, 77. (Emphasis added)

within that covenant and sacrificial system. But concerning true spiritual realities, concerning offences committed against a Holy God, the sacrifices could do nothing but point ahead to that one true sacrifice, Jesus Christ.[35]

John Owen tells us that the old covenant:

> By representing the ways and means of the accomplishment of the promise, and of that whereon all the efficacy of it unto justification and salvation of sinners doth depend. This was the death, blood-shedding oblation, or sacrifice of Christ, the promised seed. This with all its offerings and ordinances of worship directed unto; as his incarnation, with the inhabitation of God in his human nature, was typed by the tabernacle and temple. Wherefore it was far from disannulling the promise, or diverting the minds of the people of God from it, that by all means it established it and led unto it.[36]

He again says:

> Whilst the covenant of grace was contained and proposed only in the promise, before it was solemnly in the blood and sacrifice of Christ, and so legalized or established as the only rule of the worship of the church, the introduction of this other covenant on Sinai did not constitute a new way or means of righteousness, life and salvation; but believers sought for them alone by the covenant of grace as declared in the promise.[37]

When the Apostle asks why the law was given to Israel it is again the entire old covenantal system he has in mind:

> Why then the law? It was added because of transgressions, until the offspring should come to whom the promise had been made, and it was put into place through angels by an intermediary. Now an intermediary implies more than one, but God is one.

---

35. Renihan, Micah and Samuel, "Reformed Baptist Covenant Theology and Biblical Theology", 481.

36. Owen, *Works*, 22, 79.

37. Owen, *Works*, 22, 82.

The Sinaitic Covenant

> Is the law then contrary to the promises of God? Certainly not! For if a law had been given that could give life, then righteousness would indeed be by the law. But the Scriptures imprisoned everything under sin, so that the promise by faith in Jesus Christ might be given to those who believe.
>
> Now before faith came, we were held captive under the law, imprisoned until the coming faith would be revealed. So then, the law was our guardian until Christ came, in order that we might be justified by faith. (Gal.3:21–24)

These words are very instructive. The law was not meant to be permanent, it was added to, or came in alongside the promise until the formal establishment of the new covenant. It hedged Israel from the other nations to keep it separate and thus maintain the integrity of Abraham's seed (plural) until the *Seed* (singular) came. It served to ensure:

> That there should always be kept among them an open confession and visible representation of the end for which they were separated from all the nations of the world. They were not to dwell in the land merely for secular ends, and to make as it were a dumb show; but they were there maintained and preserved as evidence of the faithfulness of God in bringing forth the promised Seed in the fulness of time. So there was to be a testimony among unto that end of God whereunto they were preserved. That was the end of all the ordinances of worship, of the tabernacle, priesthood, sacrifices and ordinances.[38]

Coming in beside the pre-existing promise and being subservient to it, the law's purpose was to expose sin, to show sin for what it is, namely transgression against a holy God. In so doing it served to convince men of their sin, of their true state, and encourage them to look to the promised one for salvation.

Israel was a stiff-necked nation, always wanting to stray from the God who had saved her from Egyptian bondage and brought

---

38. Owen, *Works*, 22, 83.

her into its own land. Had God left the people to their own devices, they would have quickly become like the surrounding nations, forfeiting the very purpose of their calling:

> For had he left them to stand or fall absolutely by the terms prescribed for unto them, they might and would have utterly forfeited both the land and all the privileges they enjoyed therein. And had it so fallen out, then the great end of God in preserving them a separate people until the Seed should come, and a representation thereof among them, had been frustrated.[39]

The very manner in which the law was given to Israel speaks of the terror it served to generate in the hearts of its hearers, so much so that even Moses trembled with fear (Heb 12:21).

> By reviving the commands of the covenant of works, with the sanction of death, it put an awe in the minds of men, and set bounds unto their lusts, that they should not dare to run forth into that excess which they were naturally inclined unto. It was therefore "added because of transgressions;" that, in the declaration of God's severity against them, some bounds might be fixed unto them; for "by the law is the knowledge of sin."[40]

Again, to quote Owen, the law served to:

> ... shut up unbelievers, and such as would not seek for the righteousness, life, and salvation by the promise, under the power of the covenant of works, and curse attending it. "It concluded" or "shut up under sin," saith the apostle, Gal. iii.22.

Jesus said that is it not the healthy who need a physician but the sick (Luke 5:31), that he came not to call the righteous, but the sinful (Luke 5:32). A man who believes himself to be healthy will not seek the services of a doctor, in the same way that a man who thinks himself righteous will not flee to Christ for forgiveness. First, he must be made aware of his true condition. To this end the law

---

39. Owen, *Works*, 22, 84.
40. Owen, *Works*, 22, 81.

The Sinaitic Covenant

served a diagnostic function. The law shuts every mouth and holds all accountable to God because of their sin (Rom 3:19). It provides the sinner with "the knowledge of sin"(Rom 3:20). A good example of how the law does this is provided in chapter 7 of Romans:

> 7 What then shall we say? That the law is sin? By no means! Yet if it had not been for the law, I would not have known sin. For I would not have known what it is to covet if the law had not said, "You shall not covet." 8 But sin, seizing an opportunity through the commandment, produced in me all kinds of covetousness. For apart from the law, sin lies dead. 9 I was once alive apart from the law, but when the commandment came, sin came alive and I died. 10 The very commandment that promised life proved to be death to me. 11 For sin, seizing an opportunity through the commandment, deceived me and through it killed me. 12 So the law is holy, and the commandment is holy and righteous and good.

When Paul, or Saul as he was then known, was a Pharisee, he believed himself to be a keeper of the law. He simply did not see the true heinous nature of sin. He came to see this through the 10th commandment. Before he understood the spiritual nature of the law he considered himself alive (v.9), i.e., a good person acceptable to God. He was effectively without the law, like the rich young ruler who believed he had kept the law from his youth (Mark 10:20). Concerning mere externals Paul had much to boast about, "circumcised on the eighth day, of the people of Israel, of the tribe of Benjamin, a Hebrew of Hebrews; as to the law, a Pharisee; as to zeal, a persecutor of the church; as to righteousness under the law, blameless" (Phil 3:5–7). He considered himself "blameless" because he wrongly thought he was keeping the law. Paul knew that he had not openly coveted, in the same way he knew he had not committed adultery in the flesh, yet he failed to see that the spirit of the law goes much further, encompassing the mind as well as the body.

When, however, Paul saw what the law really required, when the commandment really hit home, he realised that in the law's eyes he was as good as dead. Knowledge of the commandment served only to convict and condemn him. Of course, this was in no way the fault of the law. Paul knew that it is "holy and righteous and good," the problem was Paul himself, he was under the law and without Christ. It was only by truly seeing himself, his sinful condition, that he came to see his need for a savior. The law, then, as Edward Fisher puts it, was:

> . . . added by way of subserviency and attendance, the better to advance and make effectual the covenant of grace; so that although the same covenant that was made with Adam was renewed on mount Sinai . . . it was not for the same purpose. For this was it that God aimed at, in making the covenant of works with man in innocency, to have that which was his due from man; but God made it with the Israelites for no other end, than that man, being thereby convinced of his weakness might flee to Christ. So that it was renewed only to help forward and introduce another and better covenant; and so to be a manuduction unto Christ, viz: to awaken the conscience, and to convince them of their own impotency, and drive them out of themselves to Christ.[41]

In this manner the law served as a tutor, or schoolteacher. It taught the nature of sin and its deserts, and, through its many types, the remedy that God was to provide. It was a disciplining force to the nation. As Gill puts it:

> . . . but besides the instruction the law gave, it made use of discipline as a schoolmaster does; it kept a strict eye and hand over them, and them close to the performance of their duty; and restrained them from many things their inclinations led them to, threatening them with death in case of disobedience, and inflicting its penalties on delinquents; hence they that were under its discipline, were through fear of death it threatened them with, all their time subject to bondage: even the sacrificial law had something awful and tremendous in it; every beast that was slain in sacrifice was not only an instruction to

41. Fisher, *A Marrow of Modern Divinity*, 63.

The Sinaitic Covenant

them that they deserved to die as that creature did; but carried in it a tacit acknowledgement and confession of their own guilt; and the whole was a handwriting of ordinances against them.[42]

If one had to summarize the function of the old covenant, it essentially did three things. First it revealed the righteous requirements of God in his law, second, it highlighted man's inability to achieve God's righteous requirements, and the consequent punishment for failing to do so, and, thirdly, it revealed the gospel in the promised Messiah, the one who would himself keep God's righteous requirements and himself pay the price for man's transgressions and sins.

Before moving on we need to briefly address the question: Which covenant did Christ fulfill? Was it the original covenant of works or the Mosaic covenant? Jesus himself said, "Do not think that I have come to abolish the Law or the Prophets, I have not come to abolish them but to fulfill them" (Matt 5:17), and Paul tells us that Jesus was "born of a woman, born under the law, to redeem those who were under the law" (Gal 4:4). From these verses one might think the answer is obvious, that Jesus was born under the Mosaic law, for is this not the law Paul speaks about in Galatians? I would suggest, however, that Jesus, for our salvation, needed to fulfill the original covenant of works, the covenant that the first Adam failed to fulfill. The Mosaic covenant was a type of the original covenant. As we have seen, it spoke of temporal earthly blessings as opposed to eternal heavenly blessings. It could never provide eternal life. The Mosaic law stipulates that all priests be born into the tribe of Levi (Num 8:16–18), but we know that Jesus was from the tribe of Judah. As the writer to the Hebrews says, "For the one of whom these things are spoken belongs to another tribe, from which no one has ever served at the altar. For it is evident that our Lord was descended from Judah, and in connection to that tribe Moses said nothing about priests" (Heb 7:13–14). Paul tells us that even with a man-made covenant, once made, "no one annuls it or adds to it once it has been ratified" (Gal 3:15). In regard to Jesus'

---

42. Gill, *A Commentary on Galatians*, 52.

priesthood we read that "when there is a change in the priesthood, there is necessarily a change in the law as well" (Heb 7:12). If then Jesus had kept the Mosaic law (the law cannot be divorced from the Mosaic covenant) for our salvation his work would have been invalid. I say this because the terms of the covenant would have been changed.

The writer to the Hebrews draws out the differences between that priesthood prescribed under Moses and Christ's priesthood, "Now if perfection had been attainable through the Levitical priesthood (for under it the people received the law), what further need would there have been for another priest to arise after the order of Melchizedek, rather than one named after the order of Aaron?" (Heb 7:11). Melchizedek is a mysterious individual, he is called "king of Salem, priest of the Most High God" (7:1), one who was also called "king of righteousness" and king of peace" (v.2). The writer uses the mystery surrounding Melchizedek to show that Christ is unlike the Levitical priests who were subject to death and had a certain genealogy, for he appeared as one "without father or mother or genealogy, having neither beginning of days not end of life, but resembling the Son of God he continues a priest forever" (Heb 7:3).

All of this served to show that Jesus' priesthood is unique, and that the law he kept for his people's spiritual redemption was not that of Moses. Some might retort to this by quoting the two verses alluded to above, namely Matthew 5:17 and Galatians 4:4. Surely these suggest that it was the Mosaic law he kept for our salvation? Both the law and the prophets bore witness to Christ (Rom 3:21). Indeed, the entire Old Testament has Jesus Christ as its center of focus and there "is typological unity in that every single part of the Old Testament, that is every single part of the Abrahamic, Mosaic, and Davidic Covenants, typologically revealed the New Covenant."[43] The law had "a shadow of the good things to come instead of the true form of these realities (Heb 10:1). It was but a copy of the heavenly realities (Heb 9:23). The Mosaic law was a

---

43. Rehihan, Samual and Micah, "Reformed Baptist Covenant Theology and Biblical Theology," 480.

The Sinaitic Covenant

copy of the law that Jesus kept for our salvation, in other words, it was a type of the original. It does not replace the original or in any way add to it. Jesus was the archetype, he fulfilled the Mosaic law in that he was the one about whom it spoke e.g. The various bloody sacrifices, while not being able to take away sin, foreshadowed Christ's sacrifice. In the moral law God revealed something of the law of the original covenant of works tailor made for Israel. It spoke of a perfection which only Jesus could achieve. It was in this sense that Jesus fulfilled the various Old Testament covenants.

Concerning Galatians 4:4, Paul does not say which law he is referring to, only that Jesus was born under law to redeem those who are under the law. I would suggest that Paul is speaking of the Mosaic law, the law he refers to throughout this letter. He is speaking of the antitype by referencing the type. If Paul only had the old covenant in mind, one would be justified in concluding that Jesus redeemed the Jews alone, for only Israel was under the old covenant law. It simply did not apply to the Gentiles, and yet, as Paul makes clear in the first three chapters of his letter to the Romans, all humanity is are under the law of God and all "have sinned and fall short of the glory of God" (Rom 3:23). The old covenant law was this universal law of God explicitly applied to a particular people. Hypothetically, if the old covenant had never been made, Jesus, to redeem his people, would still have been born under the law of God. One further point, if it was the Mosaic law which Jesus kept for his people, one would be justified in looking for the fulfilment of the this-worldly Deuteronomaic promises, rather than the better eternal promises of which the new covenant speaks.

10

The Davidic Covenant

As the coming of Christ in the flesh drew closer so the revelation became progressively clearer with the promise becoming more specific and focused.

The last of the great Old Testament covenants was that made with David. This covenant was essentially a continuation of the Abrahamic covenant of circumcision and the Mosaic covenant. While there was no formal ratification, God's dealings with David was called a covenant, as the following makes clear, 2 Chronicles 7:17–18; Psalm 89:3. As we shall see, David's family was "selected as the medium through which the promise was to take effect." It was essentially a conduit through which the Christ was to come forth. As such, the blessings, as with the Mosaic law, served as mundane types of the spiritual eternal blessings procured by Christ.[1]

Although David was made king purely as a result of God's grace, the continuation of his throne was conditional, "If his children forsake my law and do not walk according to my rules, and if they violate my statutes and do not keep my commandments then I will punish their transgressions with the rod of their iniquity with stripes" (Psa 89:30–32). Again, the Lord tells David, "If your sons keep my covenant and my testimonies that I shall teach them, their sons also forever shall sit upon the throne (Psa 132:12).

1. Pink. *Divine Covenants*, 155.

The Davidic Covenant

The conditions, as we know, were something sinful kings could not keep. Psalm 89:39–51 tells us that they soon turned their backs on the Lord and the kingship came to an end. The Lord, however, had assured David that he would remember his promise concerning the eternal nature of David's throne:

> But I will not remove him
> from my steadfast love
> or be false to my faithfulness.
> I will not violate my covenant
> or alter the word that went
> forth from my lips.
> Once for all I have sworn by my
> holiness;
> I will not lie to David.
> His offspring shall endure
> forever,
> his throne as long as the
> sun before me.
> Like the moon it shall be established forever.
> (Psalm 89:33–39)

The Lord greatly blessed David's kingship, not because of David's obedience, but on account of his grace. As Israel was given Canaan solely on account of God's grace, so David was given the kingship, and, as Israel's continuation in the land was conditional upon its obedience, so too was the continuation of David's throne. David was himself a type of the Christ, and, as Pink puts it, "like every similar transaction which occurred during the Old Testament era, it has certain typical aspects which were the figures of higher spiritual blessings."[2] David's ascension to the throne prefigured the one who was to come forth from David's line, one whose work would secure salvation for all who believed.

As David lay dying, the Lord spoke to him saying:

> When your days are fulfilled to walk with your fathers, I will raise up your offspring after you, one of your own sons, and I will establish his kingdom. He shall build a

---

2. Pink, *Divine Covenants*, 55.

> house for me, and I will establish his throne forever. I will be to him a father, and he shall be to me a son. I will not take my steadfast love from him, as I took it from him who was before you, but I will confirm him in my house and in my kingdom forever, and his throne shall be established forever. (1 Chron 17:11–15)[3]

Solomon was the immediate son, and, as we know, he built an earthly temple for the Lord, yet Solomon's house, kingdom, and throne were far from being forever. The "forever," as we have seen, was dependent on obedience. Looking back we know that this prophecy was not speaking of Solomon, but of another son, one whose kingdom and throne would last forever because of the Son of God's obedience.

Solomon started his reign well, but it was not long before he did all that was forbidden in the law. Anticipating a king, we read in Deuteronomy:

> When you enter the land the Lord your God is giving you and have taken possession of it and settled in it, and you say, "Let us set a king over us like all the nations around us," be sure to appoint over you a king the Lord your God chooses. He must be from among your fellow Israelites. Do not place a foreigner over you, one who is not an Israelite. The king, moreover, must not acquire great numbers of horses for himself or make the people return to Egypt to get more of them, for the Lord has told you, "You are not to go back that way again." He must not take many wives, or his heart will be led astray. He must not accumulate large amounts of silver and gold. (Deut 17:14–17)

Just before his death David advised and warned his son:

> When David's time to die drew near, he commanded Solomon his son, saying, "I am about to go the way of all the earth. Be strong, and show yourself a man, and keep the charge of the Lord your God, walking in his ways and keeping his statutes, his commandments, his rules, and his testimonies, as it is written in the Law of Moses,

---

3. See also 2 Samuel 7:11–16.

The Davidic Covenant

> that you may prosper in all that you do and wherever you turn, that the Lord may establish his word that he spoke concerning me, saying, 'If your sons pay close attention to their way, to walk before me in faithfulness with all their heart and with all their soul, you shall not lack a man on the throne of Israel.' (1 Kings 2:1–4)

Solomon, however, became known for his many horses, wives and his large amount of silver and gold. In regard to wives, he had 700, along with 300 concubines (1 Kings 11:4). He and his sons failed to adhere to the Lord's statutes and commandments. It is little surprise that the throne was taken from him (1 Kings 11:11). The kingship fared no better under David's other descendants. Israel found itself subject to a kind of yo-yo regime. It was subject to the ever changing vicissitudes of her kings until it finally ended up in exile. In spite of this "the LORD was not willing to destroy the house of David, because of the covenant he had made with David, and since he had promised to give a lamp to him and to his sons forever" (2 Chron 21:7).

One of David's sons, however, was unique. The prophets spoke of a son of David, one who will reign in righteousness, justice, and mercy:

> Behold, the days are coming, declares the LORD, when I will raise up for David a righteous Branch, and he shall reign as king and deal wisely, and shall execute justice and righteousness in the land. In his last days Judah will be saved, and Israel will dwell securely. And this is the name by which he will be called—The LORD is our righteousness."[4] (Jer 23:5–6).

It is appropriate that the very first gospel in the New Testament commences with the words concerning this son of promise, whom the writer refers to as "the son of David, the son of Abraham" (Matt 1:1). The one whom the law and the prophets had borne witness (Rom 3:21) had finally arrived upon the world stage. Jesus' mother was approached by the angel Gabriel who told her

---

4. See also Isa 9:6–7; Ezek 34:23–24; 37:25; Hos 3:5; Amos 9:11 etc.

that she had found favour with God and that she was going to give birth to the one promised, one would sit on David's throne forever:

> And behold, you will conceive in your womb and bear a son, and you shall call his name Jesus. He will be great and will be called the Son of the Most High. And the Lord God will give him the throne of his father David, and he will reign over the house of Jacob forever, and of his kingdom there will be no end (Luke 1:31–33).

This obedient king would do all that is necessary to fully save his people, a people who had been given to him before the earth's foundation was laid.

As we saw when we looked at the Abrahamic covenant (the same applies to the Mosaic covenant) the David covenant has a double capacity, as Jeffrey Johnson puts it: "the David Covenant must be viewed from two perspectives. Represented in the Davidic Covenant was David's natural and supernatural seed. Solomon and his descendants were David's natural seed, while Christ Jesus is David's supernatural seed."[5] As Arthur Pink opined in reference to 2 Sam 7:11–16, "the promises in 2 Sam 7:11–16 respected Solomon and his immediate successors, but in their higher and ultimate meaning, they looked forward to Christ and His kingdom."[6] However, David's natural descendants who believed in the Christ, the one who is the supernatural seed (singular), were also counted as the supernatural seeds (plural). In other words, the "supernatural seed" are all those who place their faith in the promised seed who is Christ. These are those who constitute the remnant, the Israel within Israel, the true people of God.

Where David's many physical descendants failed to keep the conditions to secure an everlasting throne, one of his descendants, the son of promise, would, through his own obedience, sit upon his throne forever. Carnal Israel knew nothing about this, they knew only a worldly kingdom based on conditions they could not

---

5. Johnson, *The Fatal Flaw*, 241.
6. Pink, *Divine Covenants*, 164.

The Davidic Covenant

fulfil, spiritual Israel, past, present, and future, on the other hand, knows a king who will reign forever.

The prophecy of old proclaimed:

> The LORD swore to David a sure oath
> from which he will not turn back:
> "One of the sons of your body
> I will set on your throne (Psa132:11).

On the Day of Pentecost this prophecy was fulfilled, with Peter declaring:

> Brothers, I may say to you with confidence about the patriarch David that he both died and was buried, and his tomb is with us to this day. Being therefore a prophet, and knowing that God had sworn with an oath to him that he would set one of his descendants on his throne, he foresaw and spoke about the resurrection of the Christ, that he was not abandoned to Hades, nor did his flesh see corruption (Acts 2:29–31).

11

Circumcision and Baptism?

IN THIS CHAPTER I will not only examine why Baptists baptize believers but also at how the Presbyterians derive their theology of infant baptism from their understanding of the covenants. This is after all, as Wright reminds us, "the primary justification for the baptizing of infants offered by Reformed Presbyterians."[1] This will involve some polemics, but it is hoped that examining what it is Reformed Baptists reject will provide the reader with a greater insight into what we do believe, in other words, looking at the negative will serve to reinforce the positive.

Many Presbyterians simply accept infant baptism as a given. Indeed, it would be no exaggeration to say that many Presbyterians cannot provide a logical explanation of doing so, as Presbyterian F. A. James puts it:

> If I may hazard a generality (a generality, however, based on years of training pastors for Presbyterian ministry), I am quite convinced most Presbyterians, whether in the pulpit or the pew, do not understand clearly why they baptize their infants. If asked to explain why Presbyterians

---

1. Wright, D. Shawn, "Baptism and the Logic of Reformed Paedobaptism," 228.

Circumcision and Baptism?

baptize infants... I would expect that many Presbyterians would stumble and blunder the explanation.[2]

Calvin suggested that the children of believers are made regenerate in the mother's womb. According to him it "is perfectly clear that those infants who are to be saved (as some are saved from an early age) are previously regenerated by the Lord. For if they bear with them an inborn corruption from their mother's womb, they must be cleansed of it before they can be admitted into God's kingdom, for nothing polluted or defiled may enter there."[3] He further added that "the children of believers are baptized not in order that they who were previously strangers to the church may then for the first time become children of God, but rather that by the blessing of the promise they already belong to the body of Christ, they are received into the church with this solemn sign."[4] According to Charles Hodge, "The status, therefore, of baptized children is not a vague or uncertain one, according to the doctrine of the Reformed Churches. They are members of the Church; they are professing Christians; they belong presumptively to the number of the elect. These propositions are true of them in the same sense in which it is true of adult professing Christians." Today's Presbyterians mostly adhere to this presumed regeneration, where the baptised child is believed to be a Christian until he/she proves otherwise.

We have seen that while Presbyterians believe there are differences in the administration of the old and new covenants, they are nevertheless one in substance or essence, being different administrations of the one covenant of grace. Robert R. Booth likens this one covenant of grace to a constitution:

> The covenant of grace is like a constitution, in that it must be administered. There is one covenant (or constitution), but there are various administrations over time.

---

2. James, F. A., "Introduction: The Covenantal Convictions of a Compassionate Calvinist," in L. B. Schenk, *The Presbyterian Doctrine of Children in the Covenant: An Historical Study of the Significance of Infant Baptism in the Presbyterian Church* (1940; reprint, Phillipsburg, NJ: P&R, 2003), xvi.

3. Calvin, *Institutes*, 4.17.17.

4. Calvin, *Institutes*, 4, 15, 22.

Reformed Baptist Covenant Theology

> Covenant administrations are similar to the various presidential administrations in the United States, each of which administers the one US constitution. Although certain amendments may be lawfully made to the constitution under a particular administration, the one constitution remains.[5]

While there is unity in that the substance of the covenant, or in the above example, the "constitution," remains the same, there is discontinuity in the changing administrations. In Israel under the old covenant, while all Israelites were considered to be covenant members, only those who believed knew the substance of the covenant or its internal spiritual efficacy; all others knew only the outward administration. The former consisted of those who had experienced a circumcision of the heart, with the latter knowing only the circumcision of the flesh.

By distinguishing between covenant members in this fashion, Presbyterians seek to justify the idea that both the regenerate and unregenerate belong to the one covenant of grace. Since the new covenant is just another administration of this same covenant, albeit, the last and fullest manifestation of it, it too must consist of the saved and unsaved. As Pascal Denault tells us:

> By distinguishing the substance from the administrations, the paedobaptists could consider a place for the non-chosen within the Covenant of Grace and thereby make a place for the natural posterity of believers. The external administration of the Covenant of Grace would, therefore, contain the regenerate and the non-regenerate, while its internal substance would contain only the regenerate. This is how, by distinguishing between the internal substance and external administration, the paedobaptists justified the mixed nature of the Covenant of Grace.[6]

Moreover, since the old covenant included children who received circumcision, the covenant sign, it seems only reasonable to assume that the new covenant, being the same in substance,

---

5. Booth, *Children of Promise*, 26.
6. Denault, *The Distinctives of Baptist Covenant Theology*, 40–41.

Circumcision and Baptism?

must also include children, and they too must receive the covenant sign, namely, baptism. As Warfield said, "God established his church in the days of Abraham and put children into it. They must remain there until He puts them out. He has nowhere put them out. They are still then members of His Church and as such entitled to its ordinances."[7]

Presbyterians have turned an analogy into an identity, maintaining that everything one can say about circumcision can equally be said about baptism. What Pierre Marcel says is typical of what most Presbyterians believe:

> *All* that we have today in our sacraments, the Jews had formally in theirs, namely, Jesus Christ and his spiritual riches. The efficacy of the sacraments of the Old Testament is *identical* with that of the sacraments of the New, because equally they are and signs, seals, and confirmations of the good will of God for the salvation of men. There is, it is true, a difference between the sacraments as regards outward appearance, but they are *identical* as regard their internal and spiritual significance. The signs have changed while *faith does not change*.[8]

In other words, what circumcision meant in the Old Testament, baptism means in the New. Marcel says that "Paedobaptists, it would seem, are so committed to the similarity of circumcision and baptism that they care little for the task of determining wherein the two are dissimilar. Circumcision is baptism and baptism is circumcision, for all theological purposes."[9] This, in the words of Jewett, involves reading "the New Testament back into the Old in a manner that violates the movement of holy history and denies the progressive of revelation."[10] Not only this, but the Scriptures make it clear that the two rites are not the same.

---

7. Warfield, "The Polemics of Infant Baptist," in *Studies in Theology* (1932) reprint, Grand Raptids: Baker, 1981. 9:408.

8. Marcel, *The Biblical Doctrine of Infant Baptism*, 86, 90. (italics in original)

9. Marcel, *The Biblical Doctrine of Infant Baptism*, 96.

10. Jewett, *Infant Baptism and the Covenant of Grace*, 97.

Reformed Baptist Covenant Theology

Many of those circumcised had unbelieving parents. Indeed, Jeremiah could say that "all the house of Israel are uncircumcised in Heart" (Jere 9:26), yet children were still being circumcised; it was a mandatory requirement. Today, however, Reformed paedobaptists only allow baptism if at least one parent believes, moreover, circumcision was only performed on male children while baptism is administered to male and females. One of the fundamental differences between credo and Reformed paedobaptists lies in the fact that the latter believe in a dual-aspect across both old and new covenants, whereas the former, the Reformed credobaptists limit any dual aspect to the old covenant. It does not occur in the new covenant.

The dual aspect in the Abrahamic covenant is not to be found in the notion of the church internal and external, but in regard to the physical and spiritual. Paedobaptists tend to neglect the physical, for example, Guy M. Richard can say about the Abrahamic covenant:

> It was not a national covenant enacted with the physical and geographical national of Israel. It was a spiritual covenant promising spiritual blessings. It was a covenant that was, at its heart, very much like the new covenant that God entered into with you and me today. To be sure, there were national aspects of the Abrahamic covenant. But these national aspects were intended by God for a spiritual fulfillment and purpose.[11]

Baptists would wholeheartedly agree with the last three lines. Everything about the covenant was geared toward "spiritual fulfillment." One cannot, however, say that the Abrahamic covenant was concerned with only temporal affairs, or only spiritual concerns. It is not a case of either/or. Circumcision had a dual role. As performed in the flesh for all but Abraham, it spoke of things temporal and earthly, yet it also suggested the possibility of things eternal and heavenly things. The spiritual aspect of the old covenant was an unknown foreign country for all Israelites, apart from those who, in faith, realized the possibility physical circumcision signposted, namely, a circumcised heart.

---

11. Richard, *Baptism*, 44.

Circumcision and Baptism?

The point made by Richard in the above quote can be disproven when one examines the credentials for circumcision, where it becomes patently obvious that circumcision was of physical and geographical import. As I have already said, it was only a seal for Abraham. For all others the rite marked entrance into a temporal covenant that spoke of earthly blessings. The criterion was entirely earthly, based on birth not faith. Genesis 17 makes it clear that the rite was to be performed on all of Abraham's seed according to the flesh. To quote Jewett, "The emphasis is entirely on this outward relationship, with no hint that one might be disqualified to receive the rite who did not personally share the faith of the patriarch."[12] Genesis 17 says nothing about faith as being the criterion for the rite. The only stipulation was that the recipients of the rite be from Abraham's physical offspring. It also included those who had been born into his household (having no physical connection) and those been purchased with money (Gen 17:13). Abraham's household must have included upwards of a hundred people, many would have known little or nothing about the rite's spiritual significance. Many, if not most, certainly did not make a profession of faith before being circumcised. An Israelite's right to be circumcised in his flesh is never called into question, if he was a member of the Israelite nation, he was entitled to receive the rite. This was irrespective of his or his parents spiritual status. This is a far cry from baptism which is not based on genealogy but faith. No one is born with the right to be baptized based on race or anything else except faith in Jesus Christ.

There is more one could say about this, but the above should suffice to show that circumcision and baptism, while being analogous, are far from being identical.

Reformed Baptists argue that the new covenant is far from being simply a "renewal" or a "fuller" revelation of the old covenant, but is, rather, an entirely different covenant. The community under the old covenant, because it was based on the genealogical principle, was mixed, whereas the new covenant community consists only of those who are regenerate. Paul makes it clear that true

---

12. Jewett, *Infant Baptism and the Covenant of Grace*, 98.

spiritual sonship of Abraham is based only on faith (Gal 3:7), and not because one can trace one's genealogical roots back to the patriarch. So while circumcision was applied to all Abraham's physical sons, baptism applies only to his spiritual sons—those of faith.

As I have emphasized throughout, our Presbyterian brothers make the mistake of equating the covenant of circumcision in Genesis 17 with the new covenant. We saw earlier that the covenant established with Abraham was of a different substance from the covenant ratified by promise with him in Genesis 15. In chapter 17 we essentially have a covenant of works, whilst in chapter 15 we have the ratification of the promise concerning the future establishment of the new covenant in Christ. Presbyterians appear to confuse these two covenants. According to Berkhof:

> The Abrahamic covenant is still in force and is essentially identical with the "new covenant" of the present dispensation. The unity and continuity of this one covenant of grace in both testaments follows from the fact that the Mediator is the same; the condition of faith is the same; and the blessings are the same, namely, regeneration, justification, spiritual gifts and eternal life.[13]

If, as Berkhof says, "the Mediator is the same" then this mediator must be Jesus. And, of course, since the only covenant of which Jesus is a mediator is the new covenant, then all who received "regeneration, justification, spiritual gifts and eternal life" did so because they were under his covenant—the new covenant. This can be expressed in syllogistic form:

Premise—Jesus Christ is the mediator of the new covenant alone

Premise—salvation is only through Jesus Christ's mediatorship.

Premise—Abraham was saved

Conclusion: Abraham was in the new covenant, under Jesus' mediatorship

Berkhof appears to be saying that the covenant established with Abraham is still in force today when in fact there was no

13. Berkhof, *Systematic Theology*, 632–33).

Circumcision and Baptism?

regeneration, justification etc., under that covenant. Moreover, if the covenant was applicable today one would expect circumcision to be necessary because this was an integral part of it. We know that the terms of an established covenant cannot be changed or annulled (Gal 3:15), yet this is exactly what Presbyterians do. What is in force today is not the Abrahamic covenant but the new covenant of which the Abrahamic covenant was but a type. While throughout the Old Testament period its ratification still lay in the future, all those who believed the promise saw beyond the types of the covenant established with Abraham in Genesis 17, and were regenerated and justified, because, like Abraham, they believed and looked to the promise, and to a "city that has foundations, whose designer and builder is God" (Heb 11:10). For example, if we take Isaac and Jacob, they were at the same time children in two senses. First, they were Abraham's natural children, but, more importantly, they were his spiritual children because of their faith:

> Thus, Isaac and Jacob were the seed of Abraham according to the flesh, separated unto the bringing forth of the Messiah after the flesh, because they were his carnal posterity; and they were also of the seed of the promise, because by their own personal faith, they were interested in the covenant of Abraham their father.[14]

John Murray asks a number of questions that highlight the paedobaptist belief in covenantal continuity:

> Are we to believe that infants in this age are excluded from that which was provided by the Abrahamic covenant? In other words, are we to believe that infants now may not properly be given the sign of that blessing which is enshrined in the new covenant? Is the new covenant in this respect less generous than was the Abrahamic? Is there less efficacy, as far as infants are concerned, in the new covenant than there was in the old? . . .[15]

---

14. Owen, *Hebrews*, Vol. 1, 121–22.
15. Murray, *Christian Baptism*, 48–49.

Reformed Baptist Covenant Theology

Murray is assuming that both covenants are fundamentally the same. Yes, it is true that the old covenant was made with the Israelites and their children, this covenant, however, was not the same covenant in which salvation is to be found. Children were only in the covenant made with Abraham's natural seed, it was a covenant based on the genealogical principle, and this was an entirely separate covenant from that promised to his spiritual seed. An Israelite living under the old covenant, being from Abraham's seed, belonged to the conditional old covenant through birth and circumcision. It does not follow, however, that a child belongs to the new covenant because he was born of particular parents. Entrance into the old covenant was by natural birth whilst entrance into the new covenant is only through a spiritual supernatural rebirth.

The purpose of the old covenant was to be a schoolmaster or guardian to lead carnal Israelites to the promised new covenant in Jesus Christ (Gal 3:24). It was only those from within the nation who obeyed the schoolmaster and looked to the promise in faith who constituted spiritual Israel. Let me emphasize again, this is what the Apostle means when he says that not "all who are descended from Israel belong to Israel, and not all are children of Abraham because they are his offspring" (Rom 9:6–7). As David Kingdom points out:

> there was a literal Israel within which there was the true Israel, so that a man could be an Israelite in the former sense without being one in the latter. There was a *de-facto* participation in the covenant, according to which a man might be circumcised of whom no more was presupposed than that he was a member of Israel 'after the flesh.'[16]

Because Abraham's physical seed belonged to the old covenant does in no way mean that the children of believers today belong in the new covenant. Let us not forget that it "is not the children of the flesh who are the children of God, but the children of the promise are counted as offspring" (Rom.9:8). The true church consists only of those who believe, these alone "are the sons of Abraham" (Gal

---

16. Kingdom, *Children of Abraham*, 33.

Circumcision and Baptism?

3:7). Yet in spite of this the Presbyterians today still seek to apply blessings upon those of the flesh because they glean a connection with fleshly Israel.

Paedobaptist Robert Lathem goes so far as to think that to deny that Israel was the church would be tantamount to a mass excommunication with the advent of the new covenant: "If the children of believers were excluded from membership in the new covenant when they had been an integral part of the old covenant, Pentecost would have been a day of mass excommunication."[17] Again, Guy M. Richard, in his recent book, which seeks to address questions on baptism, speaks of what he calls "An Incredible Silence."[18] He maintains that if circumcision had come to an end and had not been replaced by baptism, along with the blessings which the former bestowed, there would have been significant upheaval in the Christian community, "we would expect to see some kind of controversy if our brothers and sisters are right that baptism should be applied only to adult believers." Concerning the Day of Pentecost he says:

> If at 8.59 a.m. on the morning of Pentecost, the children of all those assembled in Jerusalem were considered members of the covenant community (and as such entitled to all the privileges of that membership), and then at 9.01 a.m. they were suddenly cut off from the covenant community (and as such lost all of the very privileges they had just minutes before) until and unless they professed faith for themselves, we would expect to find some kind of negative reaction.[19]

Concerning Lathem's objection, with the establishment of the new covenant, none of Abraham's true sons, those of faith who belonged to the true church, were excommunicated. How could they be? They were in Christ, united with him and made to share in his completed work, and, as we have seen, once in Christ, always in Christ. The old man in Adam is crucified. He is never coming

---

17. Lathem, *Systematic Theology*, 446.
18. Richard, *Baptism*, 91.
19. Richard, *Baptism*, 92.

back. As for the other Israel, Israel after the flesh, it was most certainly not excommunicated because it was never part of God's true church to begin with. Presbyterians can only arrive at such a conclusion because they confuse spiritual and physical Israel. As for "An Incredible Silence," there was just the opposite. Considerable controversy occurred in the early days of the church concerning the question of circumcision. This is borne out in Paul's letter to the Galatian Church.

One may ask, what privileges did a circumcised child have in the first century? He found himself under a law he could not keep, among an unfaithful community that was suffering the consequences of its disobedience by the Roman occupation. Indeed, in all probability, the child would have been circumcised by parents who were themselves unbelievers. At Pentecost, those who believed became members of a new covenant. The old covenant may have promised much upon obedience, but the reality was very different. It was a ministry of death and condemnation (2 Cor 3:6,9). It convicted of sin but provided no solution. The word the people heard at Pentecost spoke of the very thing the law failed to provide, the remedy for sin, life and freedom. Any Jew who understood this would have been glad to see the back of the old covenant because it was a burdensome yoke which they were unable to bear (Acts 15:10).

The contention that baptism replaced circumcision is wrong because the two rites are concerned with different covenants. Circumcision was only for Abraham's natural children, for all who were members of Israel according to the flesh.[20] Baptism was only instituted after the new covenant's consummation in Jesus' shed blood. It did not replace circumcision, but was to be applied only upon profession of faith. Reformed Baptists do not subscribe to so-called replacement theology. The true church was not replaced but it was expanded with the bringing in of those Gentiles who became "fellow heirs, members of the same body, and partakers in the promise in Christ Jesus through the gospel" (Eph 3:6).

---

20. Although others were circumcised who never did become part of Israel, e.g., Ishmael.

Circumcision and Baptism?

Believing the old and new covenants to be of the same substance, Presbyterians have to support the idea that, like the old the new covenant can be broken. As we all know, children who are believed to be in the covenant and are baptized all too often end up falling away—breaking the new covenant. This is a major problem because it undermines what the Scriptures say and the extent of Christ's redemptive work. According to Jeffrey Johnson:

> Placing covenant-breakers in the covenant of grace destroys the covenant. Regardless of how covenantal paedobaptists seek to explain covenant-breakers they end up doing one of two things: One, make Christ a poor Federal Head, or two, destroy the power, value and blessedness of the covenant."[21]

We are told that all those in the new covenant will know the Lord, there appears to be no exceptions:

> And no longer shall each one teach his neighbor and each his brother, saying, 'Know the Lord,' for they shall all know me, from the least of them to the greatest, declares the Lord. For I will forgive their iniquity, and I will remember their sin no more" (Jer 31:34).

This passage is unambiguous. The sins of all in the covenant will be forgiven, never again to be remembered. Presumably, then, if children are in the new covenant they must all "Know the LORD," and they should never fall away. If they could fall away God would be reneging on his promise and remembering their sins. There is no way out of this without calling into question the truthfulness of Scripture.

Moreover, the comparison that is made between the old and new covenants suggests that the latter cannot be broken:

> Behold, the days are coming, declares the LORD, when I will make a new covenant with the house of Israel and the house of Judah, not like the covenant that I made with their fathers on the day when I took them by the

---

21. Johnson, *The Fatal Flaw*, 125.

hand to bring them out of the land of Egypt, my covenant that they broke (Jer 31:31–32).

Here the LORD himself is contrasting the two covenants, showing that they are completely different. Yes, the old covenant could be, the new covenant cannot be broken. Obviously, if it can be broken the contrast would not stand, it would be like the old covenant. We have the same teaching in Jeremiah 32:39–40:

> I will give them one heart and one way, that they may fear me forever, for their own good and the good of their children after them. I will make with them an everlasting covenant, that I will not turn away from doing good to them. And I will put the fear of me in their hearts, that they may not turn from me.

Those who are in the new covenant will never turn because the Lord himself will stop them. Again, this verse is contradicted if we say that children are in the covenant, and end up rejecting Christ. To be in the new covenant is to be in Christ, there two things are synonymous. And, as Jesus himself tells us, he is the good shepherd, he leads his sheep, and they will never listen to another's voice (John 10:3–5). Why in the light of verses like this anyone would still say that the new covenant can be broken is something of a mystery to me.

Not only has Christ secured for his people eternal life, but also the very faith necessary to believe. Saving faith is the result of regeneration. The heart of stone is incapable of exercising faith, it is quite literally "dead in trespasses and sins" (Eph 2:1). First one must be given a heart of flesh, one that is alive unto God. We can say that faith itself has been earned by Christ, this is why Paul can declare, "For by grace you have been saved through faith. And this is not your own doing, it is the gift of God, not a result of works, so that no one may boast" (Eph 2:8–9). To then suggest that one can be in Christ's covenant and yet fall from that position is to call his redemptive work into question.

According to John Calvin:

Circumcision and Baptism?

> ... it is most evident that the covenant which the Lord once made with Abraham (cf. Gen. 17:14) is no less in force today for Christians than it was of old for the Jewish people, and that this word relates no less to Christians than it did to the Jews. Unless we think that Christ by his coming lessoned or curtailed the grace of the Father... Accordingly, the children of the Jews also, because they had been made heirs of his covenant and distinguished from the children of the impious, were called holy seed (Ezra 9:2; Isa 6:13). For this same reason, the children of Christians are considered holy; and even though born with only one believing parent, by the apostle's testimony they differ from the unclean children of idolaters (1 Cor. 7:14). Now seeing that the Lord, immediately after making the covenant with Abraham, commanded it to be sealed in infants by an outward sacrament (Gen. 17:12), what excuse will Christians give for not testifying and sealing their children today?[22]

The entire argument is based on the present validity of the covenant of circumcision, yet, as we have seen, the covenant made with Abraham's physical offspring no longer applies. One might well ask why the children today are not being circumcised because it was, after all, the rite enshrined in this particular covenant. Moreover, as we saw earlier, a covenant once made cannot be changed or added to, to then change the rite would be to contradict this. And, of course, if this covenant was not of grace, as many Reformed Baptists maintain, the entire argument fails.

Colossian 2:11–12 is frequently quoted is an effort to show that baptism has replaced circumcision:

> In him also you were circumcised with a circumcision made without hands, by putting off the body of the flesh, by the circumcision of Christ, having been buried with him in baptism, in which you were also raised with him through faith in the powerful working of God who raised him from the dead.

---

22. Calvin, *Institutes*, 4, 16, 5.

Reformed Baptist Covenant Theology

What exactly is the Apostle saying here? First, he is not speaking of physical circumcision because he speaks of it being carried out "without hands". By this he clearly means that it is spiritual in nature. Secondly, there is no mention here of baptism replacing circumcision, rather, he speaks of these believers being both circumcised and baptised. It seems to me that Paul is essentially saying the same as he said in Romans 6. He is speaking of the believer's union with Christ. It has nothing to do with the physical rites, but everything to do with what occurs when the believer is placed by the Spirit of God into the body of Christ. The old man is crucified, and the body of flesh is rendered powerless (Rom 6:6). Through union with Christ the believer can be said to have experienced all that Christ underwent in his death and resurrection. This is not to say that the Apostle was not thinking of what it was that both these rites symbolise. In the case of Abraham, he was circumcised to seal what had taken place in him spiritually. For all others, the rite was only a seal of belonging to the nation and a symbol of what might occur if one believed. Baptism is also a symbol, but it is as circumcision was in the case of Abraham alone, who received the rite after having believed. Only for him was the rite a seal of a circumcised heart (Gen 15:6). Baptism is never carried out as circumcision was, to suggest possibilities, but always to show what has already taken place internally, in the spiritual realm. In these words to the Colossians it is only the spiritual realm the Apostle has in mind, as Richard Barcellos comments:

> Colossians 2:11–12 is about the application of redemption to elect souls and does not imply infant baptism. If it implies anything about water baptism, it implies that it ought to be administered to those who have been circumcised of heart and vitally united to Christ through faith as a sign of these spiritual blessings.[23]

Some think that because children living after Christ's work are not in the new covenant as they were in the old, they are somehow disadvantaged. Nothing, however, could be further from the

---

23. Barcellos, "An Exegetical Appraisal of Colossians 2:11–12" in *Recovering a Covenantal Heritage*, 474.

Circumcision and Baptism?

truth. The majority of children living under the old covenant had parents with hearts of stone. They knew not the Lord, as Conner puts it, "most of these children under the Old Covenant grew up to follow in their father's footsteps and became 'covenant breakers.'"[24] If the children saw anything of the promise, it was through a very dark glass. Compare that to the children whose parents are believers today. They are thoroughly exposed to the full unadulterated gospel message. They stand in a much more privileged position.

According to Robert Booth:

> The doctrine of infant (or household) baptism is built on the unity of the covenant of grace and its various administrations. As whole-Bible Christians, we must understand God's revelation in the context of his previous redemptive revelation. Failure to do so leads to a fractured, dispensational, and disunified view of God and Scripture. [25]

The Reformed Baptists could well take this quote and apply it to their understanding of the covenant of grace. Salvation has only ever been through one mediator and one covenant of grace—the new covenant. There has never been salvation outside of Christ, no righteousness given, no remission of sins etc., these blessings have only ever been available to those who belong to the new covenant, be it by believing in the promise or by looking back to Christ's completed work. Not only does the unity shine forth from Genesis to Revelation, so too does its elegant simplicity.

The New Testament teaches us that baptism is not essential for one's salvation, this is why Paul could say, "For Christ did not send me to baptize but to preach the gospel" (1 Cor 1:17), but neither is it optional. It is part of Jesus' great commission, "Go therefore and make disciples of all nations, baptizing them in the name of the Father and of the Son and of the Holy Spirit" (Matt 28:19). Moreover, there is no ambiguity concerning who should be baptized. It is a rite to be performed only on those who already believe. As the 1689 Confession put it:

24. Conner, *Covenant Children Today*, 57.
25. Booth, *Children of the Promise*, 66.

Reformed Baptist Covenant Theology

> Those who do actually profess repentance towards God, faith in and obedience to, our Lord Jesus Christ, are the only proper subjects of this ordinance.[26]

Again, the Confession says:

> Baptism is an ordinance of the New Testament, ordained by Jesus Christ, to be unto the party baptized, a sign of his fellowship with him, in his death and resurrection; of his being engrafted into him; of remission of sins; and of giving up into God, through Jesus Christ, to live and walk in newness of life.[27]

While baptism does serve as a witness to others, its "primary significance is for the one being baptized."[28] Examples of this are seen in those baptisms carried out in a private setting, e.g., (Acts 8:36–38; 9:17–19; 16:31–34). Here baptism serves to "formalize salvation in a covenantal ceremony or transaction between God and the party baptized. It is the body of which faith is the soul. We dare not adopt, therefore, the idea that it is unimportant."[29] The rite is here reinforcing faith and instructing the believer of what the Spirit has done in uniting him to Christ.

The believer's union with Christ lies at the heart of the rite's significance. Perhaps the best passage found anywhere in Scripture which conveys this is Romans 6. Here Paul is not speaking directly of water baptism, nor is he speaking of the baptism with the Spirit which first appeared at Pentecost. In Romans, as in 1 Corinthians 12:13, he is referring to something that has always been true for the people of God, namely, that work of the Holy Spirit whereby the believer is placed into the realm of Christ, into his body, made to share in all of his redemptive accomplishments.

By understanding Romans 6 we can glean something of what it is the rite is signifying.

---

26. 1689 Baptist Confession, 29:2.

27. 1689 Baptist Confession, 29:1.

28. Waldron, *A Modern Exposition of the 1689 Baptist Confession of Faith*, 345.

29. Waldron, *A Modern Exposition*, 346.

Circumcision and Baptism?

> What shall we say then? Are we to continue in sin that grace may abound? By no means! How can we who died to sin still live in it? Do you not know that all of us who have been baptized into Christ Jesus were baptized into his death? We were buried therefore with him by baptism into death, in order that, just as Christ was raised from the dead by the glory of the Father, we too might walk in newness of life. For if we have been united with him in a death like his, we shall certainly be united with him in a resurrection like his. We know that our old self was crucified with him in order that the body of sin might be brought to nothing, so that we would no longer be enslaved to sin. For one who has died has been set free from sin. Now if we have died with Christ, we believe that we will also live with him. We know that Christ, being raised from the dead, will never die again; death no longer has dominion over him. For the death he died he died to sin, once for all, but the life he lives he lives to God. So you also must consider yourselves dead to sin and alive to God in Christ Jesus. (Rom 6:1–11)

Following what Paul had said in chapter 5:20, "Now the law came in to increase the trespass, but where sin increased, grace abounded all the more," he envisaged people saying that one should sin in order to increase God's grace. Others might have considered justification as a license for sin. Such arguments made no sense to Paul because for the Christian to live in such a manner would make no sense whatsoever. The impossibility of the Christian continuing to live in sin arises from the profound change that has taken place in his position. He was once in Adam, now he is in Jesus Christ. In Christ he has been made spiritually alive, quickened, becoming a new man, a new creation. As we saw earlier, being in Christ, the believer is where Jesus is now. Because of his identification with Jesus the believer is deemed to have gone through all that Jesus went through in his life.

It is important not to confuse the work performed by the Holy Spirit whereby we are united with Christ with what water baptism achieves. The Greek work for baptize essentially means to be plunged into, to be overwhelmed with. It does not have to refer to water, for example, John the Baptist clearly distinguished between baptism with water and baptism with the Holy Spirit (Matt 3:3). Many erroneously associate Romans 6 with water, but here, I believe, Paul is referring to yet another kind of baptism, one where believers are ingrafted into Christ by the Holy Spirit. The believer does not become dead to sin, buried with Christ and made to walk in newness of life because he has undergone water baptism, but solely because he has been engrafted into Christ by the work of the Holy Spirit. These things were true for believers long before the rite was instituted. What I mean is this, if one were to say that it is water baptism that unites believers to Christ, then all those who believed without undergoing the rite would be excluded from Christ, e.g., Abraham was certainly not baptized with water but he was united to Christ. The rite serves to symbolize that which the Spirit has done. Marking the fact that the believer is so united to Christ that he has died to one realm and been made anew in another.

12

The Distinguishing Factor

THROUGHOUT THIS WORK, I have said that both Old and New Testament believers are one in Christ; that they are both recipients of new covenant blessings. Yet, having said this, there is something that distinguishes New Testament believers from their Old Testament counterparts. So just what is this distinguishing factor? It seems to me that it is what Scripture calls the "baptism of the Spirit." This is a blessing that affects the believer's assurance and appreciation of his position in Christ. It is this that causes believers to call God "Father." Objectively speaking, believers who lived before Christ's first coming and those who live after are one and the same. Both are complete in Christ. The difference lies not in their objective position but in the realm of their subjective appreciation of what it means to be "in him."

John the Baptist declared, "I baptize you with water for repentance, but he who is coming after me is mightier than I, whose sandals I am not worthy to carry. He will baptize you with the Holy Spirit and fire" (Matt 3:11). Jesus told his disciples that after his death he would send another to be with them, "Nevertheless, I tell you the truth" it is to your advantage that I go away, for if I do not go away, the Helper will not come to you. But if I go, I will send him to you" (John 16:7). He told his disciples that following his death and resurrection they were to stay in Jerusalem and "wait for the promise of the Father", that in due course they would be "baptized with the Holy Spirit" (Acts 1:4–5). Paul tells us that they were "sealed with the promised Holy Spirit" (Eph 1:13). Clearly, this was a new thing. Of course, all believers have the Holy Spirit, not having the Spirit would mean one does not belong to Christ (Rom 8:9), for example, King David prayed that the Lord would not take his Spirit away (Psa 51:11).

What happened at Pentecost was not that the Holy Spirit came to indwell believers for the first time, but that he came in a new dimension. He came to reveal unto them a new understanding of their position in Christ, and to provide them with both assurance and power for witnessing. Believers before Christ did not call God their Father. Why not? Because they were not in possession of the Spirit of adoption. To put it simply; at Pentecost the Spirit came to endow believers with a new awareness of their adoption as sons. This gave them great assurance and empowered them for evangelism.

We are told something of what this involves in Paul's letter to the Galatians.

> I mean that the heir, as long as he is a child, is no different from a slave, though he is the owner of everything, but he is under guardians and managers until the date set by his father. In the same way we also, when we were children, were enslaved to the elementary principles of the world. But when the fullness of time had come, God sent forth his Son, born of woman, born under the law, to redeem those who were under the law, so that we might receive adoption as sons. And because you are sons, God has sent the Spirit of his Son into our hearts, crying, "Abba! Father!" So you are no longer a slave, but a son, and if a son, then an heir through God (Gal 4:1–7).

The Apostle is not here alluding to Israel *en masse*, but to believers from Israel who lived before Christ. While they were "in Christ" and heirs to the whole estate, they were treated as children under age. Indeed, they were treated like servants rather than what they actually were, sons. They too had to perform all the duties which

The Distinguishing Factor

the law of Moses required. Of course, all Old Testament believers were sons of God, they were adopted into his family, only they were unaware of what was factually true of them. As Calvin puts it: "The fathers under the Old Testament, being the sons of God, were free; but they were not in possession of freedom, while the law held the place of the tutor, and kept them under its yoke."[1]

Let me use a simple illustration to highlight the position of believers in the Old Testament. Imagine that a father owns a vast estate and that he has a son who will enter the age of inheritance when he is 21. Before he comes of age, for his own learning, his father treats him just like he does his servants. The son has to carry out the orders of those his father has employed to run the estate. Now, in actual fact, the son can be said to own the entire estate, only he does not appreciate this fact. His coming of age will not objectively change his position, but it will allow him fully enter into what is his; to enjoy his possessions in a way he was previously prevented from doing so. Let me just quote Charles Spurgeon, who says the same thing:

> Like little children, the Jewish believers were under the law. They observed this ceremony and that, just as children, even though they may be heirs to vast estates, yet, while they are in their minority, are under tutors and governors. But now in Christ we have come of age, and we have done with those school-books and that tutorship, and we have received the adoption of sons. Now, we have joy and peace in believing; we have begun to enter into our possession; we have the earnest of it already, and by-and-by we shall receive the fullness of the inheritance of the saints in light.[2]

New Testament believers can be said to have come of age, to have entered into their inheritance. By "redeem" in Galatians 4:5 Paul means delivered, not in their redemption from, although, they knew this, but rather in their deliverance from the burden of the old covenant. They were sons under age, they had the adoption, but

---

1. Calvin, *Commentaries*, Galatians 4:1.
2. Spurgeon, *Commentary on the New Testament*. Galatians 4:1–5.

they had not received the Spirit of adoption; the Spirit of God in their hearts declaring to them their coming of age, whereby they can cry "Abba! Father!" Just like the son in the illustration, the believers' metaphorically reach the age of 21 where the Father gives them the keys to the entire estate. Spurgeon expresses the essential difference between that existed between Old and New Testament believers:

> While the Jewish believers, like children, were under the law, they did not have such direct access to the Father as we have. They could not enter into such close fellowship with God as now we can. We who are the sons of God, really born into his family, feel within us a something that makes us call God, "Father," not only in prayer, saying, "Our Father, which art in heaven;" but, inwardly, when we are not in the attitude of prayer, our hearts keep on crying, "Father, Father." The Jew may say, "Abba, and the word is very sweet; but we cry, "Father," and it means the same thing.[3]

The same teaching is found in Romans 8:15–17:

> For you did not receive the spirit of slavery to fall back into fear, but you have received the Spirit of adoption as sons, by whom we cry, "Abba! Father!" The Spirit himself bears witness with our spirit that we are children of God, and if children, then heirs—heirs of God and fellow heirs with Christ, provided we suffer with him in order that we may also be glorified with him.

What does Paul mean by the "spirit of slavery to fall back into fear"? It seems to me that this is again a reference to the old covenant, but not in the way we read about in Galatians. Here he is talking about the law carrying out its primary function as referred to in Romans 3:19, "For by the works of the law no human being will be justified in his sight, since through the law comes the knowledge of sin." The ESV has employed a small 's' for "spirit of slavery" but here Paul is speaking of the Holy Spirit, the one who convicts the sinner of sin. We find Paul himself experiencing this in chapter 7:7–11,

---

3. Spurgeon, *Commentary on the New Testament*. Galatians 4:1–5.

The Distinguishing Factor

where the Spirit applied the commandment to him causing him to realize the sin in his own life.

As mentioned earlier, this blessing is called the baptism with the Holy Spirit (Acts 1:4–5). This must not, however, be confused with the Spirit baptism referred to in 1 Corinthians 12:12–13:

> For just as the body is one and has many members, and all the members of the body, though many, are one body, so it is with Christ. For in one Spirit we were all baptized into one body—Jews or Greeks, slaves or free—and all were made to drink of one Spirit.

In these verses Paul is alluding to the way the Spirit of God unites one to Christ. It is when one is engrafted into him and made to share in his redemptive benefits. This is not peculiar to New Testament believers, but has always been true of believers. Another example of this, as we have previously examined, is found in Romans 6. When Paul uses the word "baptism" in this chapter he is not alluding to water baptism, but, as in 1 Corinthians 12, to that activity of the Holy Spirit which engrafts one into the body of Christ. The chapter is about the believer's union with Christ. What Paul describes must not be thought of as simply a New Testament phenomenon, as something which only became a reality after the establishment of the new covenant. Abraham would have been baptised, immersed or engrafted into Christ as much as New Testament believers. Indeed, all, since the very first person believed the gospel promise, have been baptised into Christ's body, the church. Essentially, it means that one has been made the share in all that Jesus achieved. Jesus told those following him, "unless you eat the flesh of the Son of Man and drink his blood, you have no life in you" (John 6:53). Here he was not speaking of cannibalism or transubstantiation, but of believers being in spiritual union with him, of the believers' identification and participation in him.

In a nutshell, what occurred at Pentecost, the baptism with the Spirit, is a blessing which does not change one's position in Christ, but serves to provide one with a deeper appreciation of what one has become in Christ. Moreover, it entails more than the believer having greater knowledge of what and who he is in Christ.

Reformed Baptist Covenant Theology

Imagine a child whose father has been absent for some time and all he has to look at is a photograph. Then the time comes when his father turns up, takes him in his arms and hugs him, whispering in his ear, "you are my son, I am your father." Overcome with emotion, the child can only utter the elemental cry, Abba Father! Such is the baptism with the Spirit. It affects not only one's appreciation of who one is in Christ, but one's entire being. The child being cradled by its father for the first time experiences something far more profound than an intellectual appreciation of who his father is, it touches every fibre of the child's being; the emotions are overcome with a sense of joy that is easy for onlookers to see. Indeed, it is such that onlookers might even think that one is under the influence of too much wine (Acts 2:13).

Interestingly, water baptism and Spirit baptism are peculiar to the New Testament. The former is the outward declaration of the inner realization of the believer's union with Christ. The Old Testament believer saw the promise through a thick fog, he had no understanding about the nature of his union with Christ. For example, he would not have understood the nature of what we read in Romans 6, although it described his actual state. It is then perfectly understandable that the rite, the external declaration of the internal fact, should be instituted along with the believer's new understanding.

One last point, there has been considerable controversy about exactly when New Testament believers are baptised with the Spirit. Is there a time gap between conversion and the baptism with the Spirit? Many maintain that all are baptised upon conversion, in other words, one cannot be a Christian and not be baptised with the Spirit. Others take a different line. They say that the blessing can be given after conversion, indeed, it is often called "the second blessing." I see merit in both positions, and there are learned theologians on both sides. I will leave it for the reader to investigate this further.

Conclusion

PEOPLE TEND TO BECOME entrenched in their thinking, so I'm not expecting what I have written to change the minds of many Reformed Presbyterians, I do hope, however, that it will cause many to think about these matters.

I live in Wales, what used to be called "the land of revivals." Sadly, this epithet is no longer applicable. On average, and this has been going on for many years, one church a week is closing for good. Among the Baptists, it is one church per month, whereas, just over one hundred years ago, it was the opposite. Of course, we know that the building is not the church, but the place where the church meets. These closures are, however, symptomatic of the nation's spiritual condition. There is an awful apathy, an indifference to spiritual things. Many who do attend a place of worship are happy to attend churches where all the emphasis is on experience, or what is more appropriately called "sensationalism," at the cost of doctrine. It is not unusual for Christians to utter the line, "I don't care about doctrine." We, however, need the doctrine, and our experiences should come from a greater appreciation of who God is and what he has done for us in Christ. Anything that does not do this is a waste of time.

When doctrine is talked about one finds that covenant theology is rarely mentioned, yet it forms the skeleton upon which

God has revealed his plan of salvation. It is essential, therefore, that God's people have some understanding of this. If God is going to revive his church, and we know that this is sorely needed, Christians must return to what God has revealed to us in the Scriptures. I am not speaking of a perfunctory reading, where one simply reads a thought for the day. No, we need to become saturated with the Word. We need to know what it is to struggle to gain understanding, believing that the Holy Spirit will give us eyes to see.

It is my hope that this short book will go some way in assisting Christians to understand God's covenants. To know that there has always been only one way of salvation, one covenant of which Christ is mediator, namely, the new covenant.

Bibliography

Aquina, Thomas. *Summa Theologica*. https://www.ccel.org/a/aquinas/summa/home.html

Augustine. *City of God*, Book 15. https://www.academia.edu/29681894/City_of_God_St_Augustine_PDF_

———. *Proceedings on Pelagius*. https://www.newadvent.org/fathers/1505.htm

Barcellos, "An Exegetical Appraisal of Colossians 2:11–12" in *Recovering a Covenantal Heritage*, ed. Richard C. Barcellos, Palmdale, CA: RBAP, 2014, pp.449–76.

Bavinck, Herman. *Reformed Dogmatics*. Edited by John Bolt. Grand Rapids: Baker Academic, 2006.

Berkhof, Louis. *Systematic Theology*. Edinburgh: Banner of Truth, 1979.

Buchanan, James. *The Doctrine of Justification*. Grand Rapids: Baker, 1977.

Burgess, Anthony. *Vindiciae Legis*. Charleston, SC: Eebo Editions, Proquest, 2011.

Calvin, John. *Institutes of the Christian Religion*. Editors, John T. McNeill. Philadelphia: Westminster Press, 1960.

———. *Calvin's, Commentaries*, Galatians 4:1 . Vol. xxi Galatians. Grand Rapids, MI: Wm. B. Eerdmans, reprinted 2003.

———. *Calvin's New Testament Commentaries, Hebrews and 1 and 2 Peter*. (Translated by W. B. Johnston, A New Translation, ed. By David W. Torrance, Thomas F. Torrance), Wm. B. Eerdmans: Grand Rapids, 1963.

Chantry, Walter J. "Baptism and Covenant Theology." In *Covenant Theology: A Baptist Distinctive*, edited by Earl Blackman, 89–110. Pelham, AL: Solid Ground Books, 2013.

———. "The Covenant of Works and Grace."

Clark, *One Important Difference Between The Reformed And Some Particular Baptists: God The Son Was In, With, And Under The Types And Shadows* https://heidelblog.net/2020/03/one

Bibliography

Confessions of Faith. 1689 Baptist Confession of Faith. wwwthe1689confession.com

Conner, Alan. *Covenant Children Today.* Reformed Baptist Academic, 2007. (1657)

———. *Did the Covenant of Grace begin in the New Covenant?* https://heidelblog.net/2017/06

Cox, Nehemiah, *A Discourse of the Covenants That God Made With Men Before the Law.* In Covenant Theology From Adam To Christ, Ed. Ronald Miller, et al.., pp. 29–140.

Denault, Pascal. *The Distinctiveness of Baptist Covenant Theology: A Comparison Between Seventeenth-Century Particular Baptist and Paedobaptist Federalism.* Birmingham, Alabama: Solid Ground Christian Books, 2013.

Edwards, Jonathan. Works of President Edwards, Vol.1. New York: Leavitt & Allan, 1881.

Fisher, Edward. *The Marrow of Modern Divinity.* Swengel, PA: Reiner Publications, 1978.

Frame, John. *Systematic Theology.* Grand Rapids: P&R Publishing, 2013.

Gentry, Peter J., and Wellum, Stepen J. *Kingdom Through Covenant*, Wheaton, IL: Crossway, 2012.

Gill, John. *Gill's Body of Divinity, Vol.1.* Grand Rapids: Baker, 1978.

———. A Commentary on Galatians. Hampshire, England: Republished by BiertonParticularBaptists.co.uk

———. *Genesis 15*, Biblestudytools.com

Golding, Peter. *Covenant Theology.* Christian Focus Publications, 2004.

Grudem, Wayne. *Systematic Theology.* Inter-varsity Press, 1994.

Hodge, A.A. *Evangelical Theology.* London: Banner of Truth, 1976.

Hodge, Charles, *Commentary on Romans.* Edinburgh: Banner of Truth, 1972.

———. *Princeton Review*, October, 1853

Hoehner J. Paul. *The Covenant Theology of Jonathan Edwards*: Eugene, OR: Pickwick Publications, 2021.

Hoekema A. Anthony. *The Bible and the Future.* William B. Eerdmans, 1994.

James, A. Frank. "Introduction: The Covenantal Convictions of a Compassionate Calvinist," in L. B. Schenk, *The Presbyterian Doctrine of Children in the Covenant: An Historical Study of the Significance of Infant Baptism in the Presbyterian Church* 1940; reprint, pp. ix-xvii. Phillipsburg, NJ: P&R, 2003.

Jewett, Paul K. *Infant Baptism and the Covenant of Grace.* Eedmanns: Grand Rapids, 1980.

Johnson, Jeffrey. *The Fatal Flaw.* FGP Free Grace Press, 2010.

———. *The Kingdom of God. FGP Free Grace Press, 2014.*

Kline, G. Meredith. *By Oath Consigned.* Eerdmans, 1968.

Kingdon, David. *The Children of Abraham.* Worthing, England: Carey Publications, 1973.

———. *Encyclopaedia of Christianity.* Vol.7, 524.

Bibliography

Lann, Vander Ray, Markham, Judith, Echoes of His Presence: Stories of the Messiah from the People of His Day. Colorado Springs: Focus on the Family, 1996.
Letham, Robert. Systematic Theology. Wheaton, Illinois: Crossway, 2019.
Luther, Martin. *The Babylonian Captivity of the Church.*
Machen J. Gresham. *What is Faith.* Eerdmans: Grand Rapid, Michigan, 1925.
Marcel, Pierre-Charles. *The Biblical Doctrine of Infant Baptism.* James Clark & Co. Revised edition, 2002.
Meyer C. Jason. *The End of the Law.* Nashville, Tennessee: B&H Publishing, 2009.
Moon Joshua. *RESTITUION AD INTEGRUM. An Augustinian Reading of Jeremiah 31:31-34 in Dialogue with the Christian Tradition.* research-repository.st-andrews.ac.uk.
Murray, John. *Christian Baptism.* Phillipsburg NJ: P&R, 1980.
Neill D. Jeffrey. "The Newness of the New Covenant." In *The Case for Infant Baptism*, edited by Gregg Strawbridge, 127–55. Phillipburg, NJ: P&R, 2003.
Nichols, Greg. *Covenant Theology A Reformed and Baptistic Perspective on God's Covenants.* Birmingham AL: Solid Ground Christian Books, 2014.
Owen, John. *Works of John Owen.* Edinburgh: Banner of Truth, 1991.
Pink W. Arthur. *The Divine Covenants.* Memphis, TN: Bottom of the Hill, 2011.
Pratt L. Richard. "Infant Baptism in the New Covenant." In *The Case of Infant Baptism*, edited by Gregg Strawbridge 156–74. P&R Publishing, 2003.
Rainbow H. Jonathan. "Confessor Baptism: The Baptismal Doctrine of the Early Anabaptists." In *Believer's Baptism*, edited by Thomas R. Schreiner and Shawn D. Wright, pp.189–206. Nashville, Tennessee: B&H Academic, 2006.
Renihan, Micah and Samuel. "Reformed Baptist Covenant Theology and Biblical Theology." In Recovering a Covenantal Heritage: *Essays in Baptist Covenant Theology*, edited by Richard Barcellos, pp.475–506.Palmdale, CA: Reformed Baptist Academic Press, 2014.
Reisinger G. John. *Abraham's Four Seeds.* Frederick, MD: New Covenant Media, 1998.
Richard M. Guy. *Baptism: Answers to Common Questions.* Reformation Trust Publishing, 2019.
Robertson, O. Palmer. *The Christ of the Covenants.* Phillipsburg, NJ: P&R, 2012.
Rhodes, Jonty. *Covenants Made Simple.* Phillipsburg, NJ: P&R, 2014.
Spurgeon H. Charles. *Commentary of the New Testament.* Titus Books, 2014. Kindle Version.
———. *The Early Years.* Edinburgh: Banner of Truth, 1962.
Storms, Sam. *Kingdom Come.* Ross-shire, Scotland: Christian Focus, 2015.
Villi, Chris https://www.jesuspaidinfull.com/Documents/CVilli_1689_Federalism_Paper.pdf September 2014.
Waldron, Samuel E. *A Modern Exposition of the 1689 Baptist Confession of Faith.* Evangelical Press, 1989.

Bibliography

Wellum, J. Stephen. "Baptism and the Relationship Between the Covenants." In *Believer's Baptism*, ed. By Thomas Schreiner and Shawn D. Wright, 97–162, Nashville, TN: B&H Academic, 2006.

Westminster Confession of Faith. The Publications Committee Of The Free Presbyterian Church of Scotland. John G Eccles Printers Ltd. Inverness, 1976.

Wilhelmus a Brakel. *The Christian's Reasonable Service*, trans. Bartel Elshout, vol.1 Ligonier, PA: Soli Gloria, 1992.

Woolsey, Andrew A. "The Covenant in the Church Fathers," Haddington House Journal, 2003.

Wright, Christopher. "A Christian Approach to Old Testament Prophecy Concerning Israel," in *Jerusalem Past and Present in the Purposes of God*, edited by P.W.L. Walker. Cambridge: Cambridge University Press, 1992.

Wright, D. Shawn. "Baptism and the Logic of Reformed Paedobaptism," in *Believer's Baptism*, ed. Thomas R. Schreiner and Shawn D. Wright, 207–56. B&H Publishing, 2006.

Scripture Index

OLD TESTAMENT

Genesis

Ref	Pages
1:26	5
2:16–17	5
4:25	38
3:24	6
3:15	26, 28, 31, 37, 41, 49, 51
3:16–17	48
3:17	48
4:2–5	39
5:25	40
6:5	40
6:8	26
6:8–9	40
6:18	41
8: 20–29: 17	2
9:8–11	47
12	44, 48, 79, 83
12:1–3	43, 50
12:3	78
15	2, 27, 43, 44, 45, 46, 47, 48, 51, 78, 79, 80, 114
15:6	121
15:2–6	50
15:5	45
15:9–10	47
17	27, 43, 44, 17, 78, 79, 113,115 114
17:1	54
17:3	113
17:7	52, 83
17:6–8	57
17:8	53, 61
17:9–11	79
17:10	53
17:12	121
17:14	121
18:17–19	54
22:18	28
23	61
26:4–5	54

Exodus

Ref	Pages
2:11–22	92
6:7	83
12:5	14
16	83

Scripture Index

Exodus (*cont.*)

16:4	54
16:28	54
19:5–6	82
21:24	92
27:21	52
31:16–17	52
32:15–16	21
40:15	52

Leviticus

1:10	14
18:5	86
25:23	50

Numbers

8:16–18	99
11	83
16:46	93
20:12	93
25:13	52
35:21–22	93

Deuteronomy

17:14–15	104
27–30	87
28: 1–14	2
28: 15	2
30:6	53

Joshua

21:43–45	59
24:19	83

2 Samuel

7:11–16	104, 106
7:13–17	58

1 Kings

2:1–4	105
11:4	105
11:11	105

1 Chronicles

17:23	11–15
23:13	52

2 Chronicles

7:17–18	102
21:7	105
9:2	121

Psalms

58:3	11
51:5	11
51:11	128
89:3	102
89:30–51	103
89:30–32	102
89:33–39	103
105:10–11	60
105:44–45	60
132	2
132:11	107

Proverbs

14:34	90

Ecclesiastes

12:12	vii

Isaiah

6:13	121

Jeremiah

2:7	50
7:23	83
7:21	83
9:26	112
23:5–6	105
30:22	83
31	xi, 35
31:31	30
31:33	34
31:34	119

Scripture Index

32:39–40	120
34:18–20	47
36: 31–36	x

Ezekiel

11:20	83
36: 26–27	x
36:25–28	34

NEW TESTAMENT

Matthew

1:1	59, 105
3:3	126
3:11	127
5:17	99, 100
21:11	15
26:28	35
28:19	123

Mark

10:20	97

Luke

1:31–33	106
5:31	96
5:32	96
7:46	15
10:27	85
13:33	15
22:20	35, 89

John

1:29	14
3:2	15
5:30	12
6:37	12
6:36–40	12
6:53	131
8:44	11
8:33	72
8:34–36	72
10:3–5	120
10:14–16	12
14:6	15
16:7	127
17:6–11	12
17:17–21	12
26:28	12

Acts

1:4–5	128, 131
2:13	132
2:29–36	59
2:29–31	107
7:8	53
8:36–38	124
8:37	66
9:17–19	124
15:10	71, 118
16:31–34	124
20: 27	xii

Romans

1:7	84
2:15	39
2:28–29	69
3:2	81
3:11–16	66
3:19	97, 130
3:19–23	72
3:21	100, 105
3:23	101
3:20	80, 97
4	26
4:9–11	45
5:10	18
5:12	8
5:13–14	38
5:16	8
5:12–21	6
5:20	125
6	122, 124, 126, 131, 132
6:1–11	125
6:6	17

Scripture Index

Romans (*cont.*)

6:14	77
6:23	18, 39
7:7–11	130
7:7–12	97
8:3	7, 85
8:15–17	130
8:37–39	66
9:3	67
9:3–4	67
9:4–5	81
9:6	64, 67
9:6–7	68, 116
9:6–8	72
9:8	67, 116
9:15	68
9:24–29	68
10:4	81

1 Corinthians

1:30	16
1:17	123
7:14	121
11:25	35, 89
12	131
12:12–13	131
12:13	124

2 Corinthians

1:20	85
3:7	81
3:3–7	77
3:6	117
3:7	71
3:9	71, 81, 118
5:21	13, 19

Galatians

2:16	80
2:21	77
3:7	66, 117
3:11	80
3:13	16
3:15	79, 99, 115
3:16	64, 67
3:17	43, 44, 45, 49, 79, 114
3:18	77
3:21–24	95
3:22	96
3:24	116
3:27	64
3:29	66, 78
4:4	13, 99, 100, 101
4:1–7	128
4:5	129
4:21–31	70
5:3	53
5–6	33
6:15	64
6:15–16	57
7:5	61

Ephesians

1:4	12, 20
1:13	128
2:1	120
2:8–9	120
2:18–19	69
3:6	118

Philippians

2:7–8	12
2:6–8	13
3:5–7	97
3:8–9	19
3:20	16

Colossians

1:13	16
2:11–12	55, 57, 121, 122

Scripture Index

1 Timothy
2:5	14

Hebrews
1:13	18
6:13–18	46
8:5	89
8: 8–13	xi
8:13	52
8:6	35
7:1–2	100
7:3	100
7:11	100
7:12	100
7:13–14	99
9:9	80
8:10	31
9:9–10	89
9:25	15
10:1	100
10:12	15
10:23	100
11	26
11:2	39
11:4	39
11:6	40
11:7	40
11:9–10	61
11:10	53, 88, 115
11:13	62
11:13–16	61
11:15	40
11:16	53
12:21	96
11:22	71
12:22	62
12:25	35
13: 20	5
13:20	13

1 Peter
2:8	85
1:9	85
1:19	14
2:5	64
2:9	16

2 Peter
2:5	40

Revelation
21	61

www.ingramcontent.com/pod-product-compliance
Lightning Source LLC
Chambersburg PA
CBHW050823160426
43192CB00010B/1878